HOW TO WRITE
A CHILDREN'S BOOK

Compilation and edited by
KATIE DAVIS
Director, Institute of Children's Literature

How to Write a Children's Book

Compiled and edited by Katie Davis, Director, Institute of Children's Literature

The content contained in this guide is for informational purposes only. To be a writer you need passion and perseverance—oh, and a thick skin because people *will* tell you negative things about your ~~baby~~ book.

ISBN: 1-944743-02-2

ISBN-13: 978-1-944743-02-4

To all the writers who write to get it right

iv

CONTENTS

HOW TO WRITE
A CHILDREN'S BOOK

This book has tips on how to write and publish a book for kids and advice on writing children's books. It has been compiled and edited by Katie Davis, Director of the Institute for Writers and the associated Institute of Children's Literature. These two schools have taught over 404,000 students how to write a book for children and get published. Katie Davis is the award-winning author of the Amazon Bestseller *How to Promote Your Children's Book*.

INTRODUCTION

You want to become a better writer, and you want to learn how to write a children's book. Maybe you'd like to learn how to write for teenagers as well. This book will help introduce you to a way to do that. Much of the information is inspired by the Institute of Children's Literature (at http://institute forwriters.com) and the course (and its associated web site) that teaches writing for children and teenagers. As the director of the Institute, it's my pleasure to share some of the basics of the course and our site. Although registered students are given one-on-one guidance and instruction from published writers and editors, and can earn college credits, this guide will help you get started.

Of course, just reading a book won't teach you to write. The best way to learn to write is to read a *lot* of books in the genre and for the age level you're interested in—as many as you possibly can. The best books to read are the traditionally published bestsellers you find in bookstores, whether brick and mortar, or online. Ironic, considering this is a self-published book.

So why do I write that? Because these books are the most recent, and you know professional editors and copyeditors have worked on them. Yes, there may be wonderful self-published children's books to read, but there is no guarantee an editor has "had at them" and polished that book to a gleaming (professional level) shine.

I'd like to thank Jan Fields, one of the Institute's esteemed and talented instructors, for contributing content to this book, as well as the authors whose articles appear here, reprinted from a selection of the Institute's annual directories.

1 _____

WHERE DO YOU
GET YOUR IDEAS?

One of the most frequent questions writers are asked is, "Where do you get your ideas?" Sometimes it's cloaked in an easier form: "Where did you get the idea for that story?" But often it's a general question with tough-to-find answers. Where do we get our ideas? Does a muse whisper them in our sleep? Do we go to the idea store in Schenectady? Do we wait for some clever person to sell us an idea—offering to split the profits from the resulting book? Where do we get our ideas?

What Do the Experts Say?

Let's ask these published (and very popular) authors:

Bruce Hale: "From a small man named Guido who lives in my basement and makes them for me. No, actually. I think ideas come from the collision of two things that weren't combined before ... like geckos and mysteries. Ideas are a little bit magical, but if you keep your antennae up, they're all around you. Just ask the question, 'What if …?' and you'll get an idea rolling."

Betsy Byers: "Since my books are mostly realistic fiction, I get my ideas from the things that happen to me, to my kids, to my dogs and cats, to my friend's dogs and cats, and from things I see on TV and read about in the newspaper. I sometimes think my books are like scrapbooks of my life because almost every incident brings back a memory."

Tedd Arnold: "My ideas come from different places at different times—sometimes from something one of my children said; perhaps from seeing something outside, for example, watching animals; sometimes from just letting my mind wander. Once I have an idea, I write it down so I won't forget it. Of course, having an idea doesn't mean you have a story. Sometimes an idea immediately makes itself into a story in my head. Other times I put the idea away and forget about it. But my mind doesn't ever completely forget the interesting ideas. My mind keeps quietly playing with them. Then suddenly one day I may fit that idea into a story. Or I might combine two ideas into one story. When I have most of the story worked out in my head, I go to my paper or computer and start writing. Once in a while, I will open my folder of idea notes that I've jotted down and see if those old ideas finally spark a story. Sometimes they do. Sometimes they don't. You never know."

Holly Black: "I guess they come from things I like, my subconscious, and my past experiences. And what I wish my experiences had been. There are also movies and books that have made me feel a certain way that I want to be able to capture."

Judy Blume: "I used to be afraid to answer that question. I thought if I ever figured it out I'd never have another one!

But now I know that ideas come from everywhere—memories of my own life, incidents in my children's lives, what I see and hear and read—and most of all, from my imagination."

R. L. Stine: "*Goosebumps* fans are always asking me that question. And it's not an easy one to answer. Think about where you get your own ideas. They come from everywhere. People you meet. Stories. Movies. Dreams. Memories. Thin air!"

Robin McKinley: "The short answer is: I haven't a clue."

Jane Yolen: "I am always asked where I get my ideas from. That is a very difficult question to answer, since I get my ideas from everywhere: from things I hear and things I see, from books and songs and newspapers and paintings and conversations—and even from dreams. The storyteller in me asks: what if? And when I try to answer that, a story begins."

So Where *Do* Ideas Come From?

Ideas come from ...

Freedom: When we give ourselves permission to daydream; when we value our down time and the free flow of thoughts, we invite in ideas.

Observation: The world is filled with ideas—even Schenectady—and we need to slow down and look, listen, observe ... to find the idea store nearest you.

Questioning: Let yourself be a kid again, filled with questions and musings and even wishes: "What if ... ?" "I wonder ... " "I wish ... " Let the questions take you to places where ideas live and grow.

5

Grouping: Neil Gaiman says sometimes his ideas come from putting together things that don't normally go together: "If a person bitten by a werewolf turns into a wolf, what happens when a goldfish is bitten by a werewolf?"

How Do You Know When An Idea Is Worth Following?

We have ideas all day long—daydreaming, wishing, rewriting the last argument we had with a family member. Most of those ideas aren't stories. But how do you tell which ones are? A story is an idea that grows until it takes on a life and energy of its own. That doesn't mean a story idea doesn't sometimes bog down or thin out or take sweat to bring to conclusion. It means you grab hold of energy and excitement when you take off. One writer says it becomes more like dictation than creation. When you have a story, the people in it become real to you—which is key—because an idea without convincing characters is just a notion, not a story. And once you're convinced by the characters, then their responses and voice grow out of that life and energy. It can sound mystical. It can feel mystical. But ultimately it's a marriage of the freedom you've given your mind to wander and question, and the order you bring upon it during the writing process.

Never Dumb It Down

Jan Fields is one of our long-standing instructors at the Institute of Children's Literature, and she had this to say about "dumbing down":

I read a lot of writing boards and writing email lists. These places have given me unexpected networking opportunities and made me aware of new markets. They're well worth the time I invest. They also sometimes drive me crazy. The one thing that most frequently makes me tense is when I see someone react to a rejection or critique by grumbling, "I guess I'll never be published for kids because I just refuse to dumb down my writing."

Published children's writers don't dumb down their work––ever. "Dumbing down" means condescending to the reader, and the second anyone tried that, his/her chance of publication would be virtually nil. Some children's writers craft work that is intentionally challenging—work that embraces deep themes and complex ideas. But themes and ideas are never what the message board grumblers mean when they insist they won't "dumb down."

Invariably, those folks are talking about approach, word choice, structure, pace, or vocabulary. What they mean is that they want to write for children and teens in exactly the same voice they would use to write an academic treatise or a literary adult novel. What they mean is that they don't want to do the work of capturing an authentic voice that connects with a reader who is not them. What they mean is that they don't want to do the work, and they don't want to take the blame either. They insist the blame lies in publishing that demands they "dumb down."

But publishers don't want them to dumb down. Many times I have heard editors and agents say they're looking for smart books or smart humor. But smart doesn't mean academic. Smart doesn't mean dry. Smart doesn't mean trying to force your reader to like what you like. Smart doesn't equal middle-aged.

Smart Books Connect

Books can be challenging. *Harry Potter* challenged younger readers to stick with a thick book from beginning to end. *A Single Shard* challenged readers to explore a culture that was different from theirs. *Loser* challenged readers to think about the way they look at kids who are different. *Holes* challenged

7

readers to follow several distinctly different storylines and viewpoints and to have the patience to wait for them to connect. None of these books was dumb, but all of them were authentic.

Kids can tell when they're being talked down to—they can also tell when you haven't done the work of understanding their culture, their viewpoint, and their interests. Can you imagine being asked to write a book set in a culture substantially different from your own, one that uses English but in a different way from how you use it? Now imagine doing that with zero time spent actually looking at that culture. Imagine just assuming they should accept how you do things or else they're stupid. Do you think you could land publication for that book?

This doesn't mean you need to learn all the trendy slang. Trendy slang will date your work, and many publishers are leery about that. But it does mean your characters need to sound like kids, think like kids, and (to mention a very basic thing) have names that real kids have. Names? Sound like an odd thing to mention? Editors say one of the quickest ways they can tell if an author is out of touch with real kids is if they see characters named Sally, Betty, John, and Richard—in other words, names that you just don't see in schools today. Your story will actually feel more authentic with a completely made up name like Desinique than with a name like Sally.

So what are some of the ways writers can fail to connect with readers?

- Overly formal word choices
- Overly formal sentence structure
- Long monologues

Again, the problem isn't that readers wouldn't know what a formal word means or cannot follow a formal sentence structure. It's because they won't believe you if you use them. They won't believe in a bunch of teens who talk like middle-aged lawyers. They won't believe in a bunch of young children who launch into long soliloquies about duty, emotion, morality, or pretty much anything else. If they don't believe you, you've lost the chance to make your story connect.

Smart Books Provoke

Another thing you can do without ever dumbing down is provoke readers to think. Smart writing doesn't try to raise someone else's child. Smart writing doesn't tell kids what to think. Smart writing just coaxes them to think about something new or sometimes something very familiar in a totally new way. It draws readers out of the day-to-day rut of thinking about just those things under the reader's nose and expands the world.

A smart book might provoke the reader to think about injustice—what is it really? Might it be something different than we think? Can it be hidden by calling it something else? A smart book might provoke the reader to think about power—what is it? How does it affect your choices and actions? Is it a good thing or a bad thing? Smart books get the reader to ask the questions, to think—explore—examine. It doesn't tell the reader what to think but provokes the reader to think.

But ... but ... but ... what if they don't get it? Shouldn't we be trying to show them what to do in order to be a positive part of society?

Smart Books Respect

A smart book respects the reader's ability to think and make wise choices when presented with sufficient

9

perspective. A smart book recognizes that just because a reader uses contractions, speaks in bursts instead of monologues, and has developed a whole language to simplify typing with his/her thumbs doesn't mean there is anything wrong with that person's brain. A smart book knows you learn more by working out a problem than by being told the solution.

At the end of a smart book, the plot is brought to a satisfying ending, but the thinking has just begun. A smart book respects that thought process, and a smart writer sets aside agenda, ego, and laziness to do what it takes to write a smart book. There's nothing dumb about that.

Getting the Work Done

The rewards of writing are great, but it's not always easy to do and *very* easy to put off! You'll need to discipline yourself, developing the same work attitudes of professional writers. You need to plan and stick to a regular writing schedule, to meet deadlines, and to prepare your manuscripts carefully and professionally.

I recommend that you set aside some definite hours every day to do your work. A fixed time schedule ensures that you proceed at a steady pace, with results you can see from week to week. Figure out when your best thinking time is. Are you a morning person or a night owl? It's especially important in distance learning to adhere to a planned schedule—a realistic one that you devise yourself. Start thinking now about how much time you'll be able to spend on your reading (books in your genre) and writing. The pace you set will determine the total length of time you'll need to complete your book.

2 _____

HOW OLD IS YOUR READER?

Contributed by the late author Elaine Marie Alphin, former Institute of Children's Literature instructor

I couldn't get the character out of my imagination. Maria stood in a crowded outdoor market, looking up at a sad-faced man and woman who reached for the worn teddy bear she clutched. Why was the girl considering giving her bear away? Would she go through with it?

Somehow I felt compelled to write her story. I love teddy bears, and I knew only dire circumstances could have forced me to consider giving up my childhood bear. I imagined this girl as living in El Salvador during the guerrilla war. Letters from my grandmother in El Salvador had made me feel the desperation of families caught between guerrilla and rebel soldiers.

Because I'm drawn to middle graders, I made Maria the 12-year-old heroine of a story called "A Market Day to

Rejoice." She was excited about helping her father barter for much-needed food at the market, only to face the question of whether to trade her beloved teddy bear.

But was this really a middle-grade story? Children clutching teddy bears tend to be younger than 12. Could middle-grade readers believe that Maria would care so deeply about her bear? Reluctantly, I realized the answer was probably no. I rewrote the story for beginning readers, making Maria several years younger. I thought youngsters in the six-to-nine age group would not only identify with Maria's love for her bear but would also understand the strength she'd need to give it up for the sake of food for her family— and for the comfort of an unknown little boy who had been hurt by soldiers in an ambush. My editor at HarperCollins agreed, and *A Bear for Miguel* was published as an *I Can Read* book. I didn't sit down to write this story for primary graders, but I discovered they were the right readers for the story I wanted to tell.

Zeroing in on an Age Group

Should you decide you're going to write for a particular age group and then come up with an idea that fits them? Or should you decide to write a story or article about a particular idea, then choose the age group that's right for it?

Actually, it can work either way. From my first stories and articles for children, I always began by thinking in terms of my favorite audience—intermediate readers. These young-sters have developed strong reading skills, so I can use a full range of vocabulary and syntax for them, but they also have active imaginations, which makes them fun to write for. As I did with "A Market Day to Rejoice" in its original form, however, I have to ask myself: Will intermediate readers be interested in this idea? Will they identify with this character? Can they imagine themselves in this situation? If not, I need to redirect my story to a more appropriate age group.

At other times, I just get a wonderful idea and then ask myself which age group would be most interested in reading about it. When I got the idea for a story about a rambunctious boy who discovers the importance of apologizing when he bumps into a girl in his rush to grab a cupcake from the after-church snack table, I could visualize an energetic eight-year-old reading the story and remembering the last time he ran through the community hall. I wrote "Truly Sorry" and saw it published in two primary-grade magazines.

Know Your Reader's Birthdate

From whichever direction I approach the question of age targeting, I've discovered that the important thing is to settle on the best readership for my story or article before I put the first word down on paper. This decision determines the way I approach my fiction theme, the behavior and language of my characters, the way I focus a nonfiction article, and the depth of my research. In addition to the vital matter of length, the choice of readership age also determines my writing style in terms of syntax, sentence structure, and vocabulary.

This was brought home to me vividly when I decided to change my target readership for Maria and her bear—and found I had to rethink the manuscript completely and rewrite it from scratch! For example, one paragraph in my version for middle graders read:

Papa found a man who was interested in his tools, and got a fine new frying pan for Mama, and the promise of two chickens. The man also knew someone who might be able to use Papa to do some extra repair jobs. Maria watched the wagon while Papa went to talk to the man.

In the version for primary graders, I handled the same section differently:

Then a man talked to Papa. "This man will trade two chickens and a fine new frying pan for my tools," Papa told Maria. "He also knows a farmer. I must talk to him about some work."

"What about the milk?" Maria asked. "And the butter and eggs?"

Papa laughed and said, "Don't worry, Maria. You make a good trade for me!"

For primary graders I used shorter paragraphs, simpler words, and lots more dialogue to keep the readers involved. I also let Maria be younger and more anxious about the situation.

In fiction, the age of your main character determines the age of your readership. Children want to read about someone who's their own age or a little older and see what they might become in a few years. I knew if I were going to write about Maria for middle graders, I'd have to make her 12 in order to interest them—and to interest the editors who publish for these readers. But it's not enough to say that a character must be 12 because you want to write for intermediate readers! She must behave and sound like a 12-year-old. Most important, she must be in a situation that other 12-year-olds will identify with. That's where I ran into trouble with Maria and her teddy bear.

I learned from experience that before you develop a story idea for a particular age group, it's important to imagine a child at the upper limit of that age range reading your manuscript. Will she be interested? Will he think it's babyish? Will the idea be relevant to that imaginary reader? If not, I either change my idea until it works for that reader or try writing it for a different age group.

Nonfiction: Ages and Stages

I ask myself the same questions about article ideas. Almost anything can become a nonfiction topic for young readers, given their curiosity and appetite for facts about the world around them. But each topic has to be aimed at the right readership. For example, I knew the subject of flying fish could make a wonderful article, but for which age group? Middle graders would probably already have learned about these creatures in school, I reasoned, whereas the idea of a flying fish would come as a surprise to primary graders. Surprises sell—and so did "Sea Breeze Escape," to *Spider*.

Hitting the Mark with Preschoolers

Children discover the world around them one step at a time, something I keep in mind as I decide which readers to target. Let's say I want to write about insects—kids of all ages love bugs. If I target preschoolers, I'll build on the fact that their immediate surroundings—their homes, streets, yards—are full of wonders they're just beginning to discover. How about a common insect like the ant as a topic for these readers? I needn't do complex research, just present a few basic facts simply and clearly. But this is a satisfying kind of writing, since an intriguing introduction to ants will prepare children to learn about insect communities, the food chain, and more sophisticated insect relationships as they grow older. A simple article for young listeners can spark a lifelong interest in entomology.

Enticing Beginning Readers

What aspect of insects would appeal to primary graders? As these readers leave home to start school, they're discovering independence and beginning to question the world around them. Parents may have warned them that spiders can be dangerous—but do adults have all the answers? An article contrasting poisonous spiders with beneficial spiders that eat common household pests will invite your reader to question basic assumptions and stimulate curiosity to learn more.

I won't try to cover too much ground, though, knowing that if you give six- to-nine-year-olds too many facts leading in diverse directions, you'll overwhelm them. Instead, I'll keep my information manageable, knowing they can pursue it in more depth as their reading abilities develop. That's the great joy of writing for these readers—as they discover the wonders of reading, they realize there's a wide world out there to explore. Whether I write about spiders or flying fish or dinosaurs, I know I'm introducing them to a topic that may become a passion by the time they grow into middle graders and begin to embrace those subjects that interest them.

More Gore for Middle Graders

And those middle-grade readers love facts! They want to know everything, the better to recite more—and quirkier—facts than their friends. They especially like yucky topics that make adults cringe. When I decided to write about insects for these readers, I chose the dermestid beetle as a topic—a beetle that eats the flesh from animal bones for natural history museum displays. Gruesome, you say? Absolutely! Middle graders enjoy gruesome. I knew they'd want to know things like how long it would take a colony of beetles to clean a moose carcass, as opposed to that of a bat. They'd want to know where the beetles live in between eating sessions, and what they eat when there aren't any bones handy.

But I didn't rewrite the encyclopedia for them. They can read that for themselves. I kept "Beetle Bones" focused on the museum uses of this quirky bug. Nor did I tell them whether they should think this idea was good or bad. Intermediate readers like to sift through the facts and draw their own conclusions.

They also like to get in on the action themselves, so a project or activity can increase the appeal and marketability of an article for this age group. A sidebar might show them how to build their own insect habitat, for instance. But middle graders are impatient to learn quickly, without fuss. I knew they wouldn't sit still for a graceful prose description of a dermestid beetle in its natural habitat—for any kind of description, in fact. But adolescents will.

Present the Real World to Adolescents and Young Adults

Ten- to 14-year-olds don't like to think of themselves as kids any longer. They want to confront adult problems and find solutions. If there's a rare insect in danger of extinction in the South American rain forest, adolescents will be interested in reading about the fight to save it. In writing about this topic for these readers, I'll start with facts to document the threat to the insect, then go on to describe its environment in detail and also show readers how to get involved in the fight to save it. Adolescents crave intense situations. They want to find ways to save the world, and they're willing to learn anything that will help them achieve their quest.

While adolescents long to be grown up, young adults are almost there. Since most will have studied entomology at school, I don't need to fill my article with textbook information. Instead, I'll look for ways to make bugs relevant to their lives. For older teens about to rent their first apartments, I might write about the resilience of cockroaches, including the reasons why they're unhealthy as well as distressing to have around, and suggest ways to combat them in an apartment building. Or I might interest young adults in career possibilities in entomology by interviewing a scientist who's made a discovery, and focusing on research programs at his university.

Enter a Wide-Open Nonfiction Market

Writing effective nonfiction is at heart a matter of matching readership to topic. You can begin with any general subject area that fascinates you, then size it to an age group by identifying an aspect of the subject that will appeal strongly to that group's interests. Editors publish more magazine articles than fiction, and they're constantly in need of creative articles that introduce young readers to new topics—an invitation for new writers eager to break into print.

Writing nonfiction can also introduce a writer to an editor and lead to sales in other genres. I wrote nonfiction for the Cricket group of magazines for years before selling them my first fiction piece. A writer who can come up with entertaining nonfiction ideas for different age groups will impress editors and build a strong list of published credits.

Fiction Targeting: Middle-Grade Concerns and Conflicts

Perhaps you know you want to write stories for a certain readership, the way I'm drawn to middle-grade readers. No matter how hard you try, your characters insist on being primary graders or adolescents. But how well do you really know your age group? I stay close to the concerns and psychology of my own target readership by taking time to observe middle graders as individuals and reading magazines and books that are published for them.

Watching middle graders is the first step toward thinking like them. These youngsters are turning away from family to friends, and right and wrong seem inextricably mixed with

18

peer pressure. Their struggle to achieve independence and self-confidence often puts them at odds with either parents or friends—lots of potential conflict for stories as they struggle to balance these tensions! I've written a story about two middle graders who rescue injured wildlife over their parents' protests; a book about a girl who solves a hundred-year-old murder mystery by relying on family bonds and loyal friends; and another book about a boy who finds his self-esteem when he helps a ghost find a family heirloom.

Observation also yields concrete detail that will make an imagined story situation come alive. All children go to school, but middle graders study certain subjects. Use these in your stories. For example, your main character isn't just worried about a tough teacher, he's worried that his teacher will flunk him in medieval history while his friends all pass, and he won't get to take part in the medieval fair. Or perhaps he's worried because he finds the Middle Ages a breeze and he's acing the tests while his friends are failing. Should he deliberately fail a test to fit in, or is it worth standing out in order to prove to his parents that he can earn better grades when he's studying something he really likes?

Outside the classroom, middle graders play sports competitively. You can build a story around an intense soccer game or a clique within the swimming team—whatever sport interests you. Kids this age are also old enough to stay home alone, and even baby-sit younger children. Ask yourself what trouble they could get into without an adult around, and how they might deal with it.

When you think trouble, though, be aware that the market sets limits on scary situations and graphic detail for middle graders. These readers love a taste of danger, but while a mystery or adventure story for this age group can involve a degree of violence, editors prefer that kids not confront a violent adult by themselves. When Jessica solved the ancient murder mystery in my novel *Tournament of Time*, I had her use the ghost of the other adult suspect to defeat the murderer's spirit. If she'd had to outsmart a kid villain, I'd have let her face the culprit on her own.

I've found that reading editorial guidelines can also generate age-appropriate ideas. Editors may have specific needs for middle-grade stories set at camp, for stories about characters with disabilities, for urban settings, or for particular genres, such as adventure stories, science fiction, mysteries, or historical fiction. By combining such timeless middle-grade issues as friendship, competition, and approaching maturity with these specific needs, I can be sure of creating intermediate fiction an editor will be interested in reading.

Fiction Targeting: Other Age Groups

Use the same techniques of observation and reading to get a feel for the way editors see children in other age groups.

Preschoolers

Writers who observe and write for preschoolers know that these children worry about new babies, and whether their parents will always love them even if they do something wrong. They want to play with flowers and grass and butterflies and stuffed animals and wooden cars—whether the toys are theirs or belong to someone else! They're curious about the colors and shapes and sounds of their immediate world. This world can be as close as their backyards or day-care centers, or as far away as the realms of their imaginations.

Creating age-appealing characters for this age group is no problem, since everyone is older than a preschooler! They're eager to grow up, and they want to read about characters who are mastering the skills they struggle with—not just physical challenges, but also social skills.

Like many other writers, I often use animal characters for this age group. For example, Elephant wants to have dinner with his friends, and can't understand why they're all avoiding him. Then he remembers how he gobbled up Baboon's berries and crunched Warthog's carrots and Hippo's lettuce—everything his friends brought to their last dinner party! So he puts together his own feast of oranges and breadfruit and invites his friends to share it. Along with Elephant, the child discovers the importance of sharing—an enjoyable lesson in story form. The plot is simple and easy to follow, and I used lots of dialogue and action.

Here are some other simple plots I've used for preschoolers:

- A girl uses her doll to meet the preschooler next door.

- A boy helps his father do household chores, and in the process finds Dad's glasses.

- A girl finds a way to make the most of a snowy day after everyone tells her she's too little to help them shovel the driveway or build a snow fort. She even graciously allows them to help her when they discover she's big enough to make something special after all: a snow rabbit.

Primary Graders

Primary graders are entering the wider world of school and independence. Watch them play, and you'll see them striving to work things out by themselves before running to parents or teachers for help. Stories for this age group can show them experimenting with different sports or sorting out friendships at school. Characters may struggle to balance their wishes and needs against the needs of family and/or other children, as in the case of my character Maria, caught between the desire to keep her teddy bear and her family's need for food.

Six- to nine-year-old readers can enjoy talking animal stories, as long as the animals have quirky personalities and deal with the same kinds of real-life problems readers face. But mostly they like to read about children their own age or a bit older. Here are some situations I've used in stories for primary graders:

- A boy getting his school picture taken is tired of having a "family face," but discovers that genetic inheritance from his family can make him special too.

- A second grader whose mother returns to college wonders how she can still feel secure about her family life.

- A boy prays for a birthday puppy, to his mother's dismay, then reassures her that God always answers prayers—even when the answer is no.

Adolescents

Stories for adolescents move beyond home and school into a larger community of peers and the world of romance. While editors don't want to see sex in stories for young teens, these readers are wondering about it. No longer are these youngsters torn only between family and friends—now they have to factor dating into their web of relationships, balancing their hormones against parents' admonitions, and perhaps against their promises to friends as well.

Their bodies are telling them they're adults, while the rest of the world is telling them they're still children. As a result, they want to read about characters who confront dramatic situations and prove their adulthood in the process. In addition to sex, they're concerned about gangs, drugs, and school violence. In this new world of adolescence, sadly, punishment for wrongdoing is more likely to entail arrest than staying after school.

Sometimes a character I've conceived as a middle-grade protagonist will turn out to be an adolescent. This happened with Kevin, the hero of my novel *The Proving Ground*. The son of an Army officer, Kevin was starting a new school in a town that despised the military. But on page 1, he saw a girl he completely fell for. And he didn't just run into problems at school—he ran into hostility from the entire community that would culminate in his having to confront an armed teenage terrorist in a life-threatening climax.

This went way beyond intermediate material! Instead of having Kevin start middle school, I let him start high school. His romance would be stormy, because the girl had special reasons to hate the military. And he would have to go against every rule his father had set, putting himself at risk to save the deserted military base from the terrorist attack. At the same time, Kevin was still a youngster, with a pet hamster he was determined to protect. He respected his parents even as he made his own choices about what was right for him to do. And as much as he liked the girl, his romance never went beyond intense friendship—appropriate for adolescent readers.

Young Adults

Young adults are, as the name implies, on the brink of adulthood. Older teen characters typically work through such questions as whether to try college or to get married and start a career. They may face the consequences of an unwanted pregnancy.

They may own cars (they can certainly drive them), and have jobs when they're not in class.

It's difficult to write fiction for them, because most of them read adult fiction—mysteries, romances, science fiction, and horror from the adult shelves. They want to read about complex issues that don't have easy answers. Writers who tackle this age group need to read sample publications carefully to get a feel for what different editors are looking for.

My own teen fiction includes a story about a young man whose small brother prayed nightly to Baby Jesus for a sled for Christmas—a gift the family could not afford. The protagonist worked to earn money and skimped on other gifts so that his brother's prayer would be answered. That would have made a good story for adolescents, but for young adult readers I didn't stop there. The little brother was so delighted with his present that he returned unnoticed to the church creche and took the Baby Jesus for a sled ride. When the adult members of the congregation suspected gang-related vandalism, the teen's challenge was to show them how to understand and share his brother's pure faith and joy in God's Son.

Here are some other ideas I've used for young adult readers:

- When a group of teens tries to help homeless families, a boy is forced to accept the reality of his divorced father's homelessness.

- A girl and her boyfriend mock the outcast girl in class by sending her a black carnation for Valentine's Day. The girl later regrets it, but discovers that apologizing doesn't make everything all right.

Issues are complex for these readers, and writers should be willing to face hard questions, not settle for easy solutions.

Which Readership Is Right for You?

If you can imagine writing for several different age groups and don't know which to choose for your first tries at publication, consider market demand. The greater the market opportunities, the better a new writer's chance of being published. These opportunities fluctuate with time, of course, but it's safe to say that manuscripts for beginning readers and middle graders will always be in strong demand. Magazine editors publish a broad range of fiction and nonfiction for these two age groups.

On the other hand, the market for preschoolers can be difficult to crack, as editors look critically for deceptively simple fiction and nonfiction that will appeal to parents and children alike.

And if you're considering writing for adolescents and teens, you should be aware that editors generally publish more nonfiction than fiction for these age groups.

Finally, think back to your own childhood. Do you have to strain to remember some years, while others are more vivid in your mind than what you did at work yesterday? Those vivid years probably signal the age level you'll write for most often. The deep emotions in your memories will make your writing resonate with young readers who share the same passions, fears, and hopes you experienced at their age.

But don't feel you have to commit yourself to a particular age group right away. You may want to write a primary-grade story inspired by your grandson, and then turn around and write a how-to article for middle graders based on one of your favorite crafts. Many writers take years to discover the niche that's right for them. Meanwhile, they have fun experimenting with writing for different readerships.

Maria's plight struck a chord within me. I could feel her conflict—her worry about her family and her love for a special bear. It made me wonder if I could have given up my most prized possession to help my family. When primary-grade readers of *A Bear for Miguel* tell me the same thing, I know I found the right audience.

3 _____

WRITING BASICS

If this has happened to you before then you're like many writers. You want to write, write, write! In fact, you feel such an overwhelming urge to express yourself you want to write it all down on paper—convinced that you have a story to tell. Or maybe a character is "talking" to you. But then you sit in front of your keyboard, staring at that blank screen, or with your hand poised over a clean, white sheet of paper, and your mind comes up with nothing. You conjure up phrases and discard them; you write an opening paragraph, reread it, and scrap it in disgust; you stare out the window, then get up to make a cup of tea or check to see if you got any email. Your solid idea has evaporated into thin air.

When you were in school did your teacher ever give you permission to write on anything you wanted? Or create a story from thin air? Then what happened? Every single fantastic or interesting thought was sent running right of your head, right? This is why writing prompts are so wonderful! They trigger an idea, like pressing the accelerator in your car.

A topic idea can get you started just as though someone had done a little pre-thinking for you and pretty soon, the writing starts to flow.

How To Get Going

Just like back in the day (don't ask how far back or which day...) when you were in school getting writing prompts, I'm going to give you one right now. Take a look at the pictures that follow. Select one based on the age group you're interested in writing for, and write a 500-to-1,000-word story, using the picture as your inspiration.

Writing Prompts

Remember that accelerator pedal that was your pre-thinking mechanism? The visual provided is going to act as a writing prompt for you. On the next few pages, you'll find illustrations for three potential stories. The pictures represent three different situations and with different main characters. Each will appeal to a different age range. One picture involves anthropomorphic animals, which is simply animals behaving like human beings. It's been popular in children's stories for generations. Just think of *Goldilocks and the Three Bears*. The second picture shows a girl in the woods; the third involves a teenaged boy sitting by a drain with a skateboard.

Study the pictures and select the one that appeals to you most in terms of subject matter and age level. Young readers' age groups may be roughly broken down into youngest listeners/readers (ages 3–7), intermediate readers (ages 8–12), and teen readers (ages 13–18).

As you look at the pictures think about which young person—or animal—might become your story's main character, the one around whom you'll center the action.

Three things to remember

1. Don't forget that children and teenagers are more interested in reading about other kids than they are in reading about adults. Children will identify with another child, *not* a grownup, so resist the temptation to give an adult character center stage!

2. *Really* resist the desire to teach a lesson. There is nothing more deadly to a story than a pedantic moralistic tale.

3. Lastly, unless you are well-versed (Yes, pun intended!) in meter and rhythm, please leave the rhyming to Dr. Seuss. It may seem easy, but the number one dead giveaway that a children's writer is a novice is that early effort to be the next Dr. S!

Pick one of the pictures that follow. Below each picture, you'll find a list of questions to think about as you consider your choice.

- Where are the dogs going?
- Are they returning or on their way?
- Can you find something in the picture suggesting a problem or conflict that needs to be solved?
- How is the cat involved in the situation?
- Which animal might be the main character in this story?

What do the other details in the picture suggest about the setting, the time, the events?

- What emotion is the boy feeling and why?

- What might you infer about his mood and personality?

- What might you infer about his relationship to others?

- What problem or conflict does the scene suggest?

What time of day, season of year, and geographical location are suggested by the other details in the picture?

- Why is the girl just sitting in the middle of the forest?

- What is she dressed up for?

- What problem or conflict does this scene suggest?

- Why is the girl looking to her right?

- Could someone else be the main character, someone "off camera"?

- What do the other details suggest about the time of year, the weather, the type and location of the woods?

Now, what do you think is going on in the picture you've chosen? What events might have led up to that particular scene? What might be about to happen next?

Don't forget, that picture only exists as a writing prompt, to help you get started on your story—your potential young reader will not have seen it. That being the case, your story has to be able to stand on its own. Don't feel forced to use everything in the picture, or even "match" the scene at all in your story if your ideas lead you in a different direction. Just use the picture elements that interest you and continue on from there.

As you begin piecing together a story in your mind, ask yourself:

- Am I really comfortable trying to write something about this subject?

- Would I feel more at ease, perhaps, writing for older (or younger) children?

- Do I feel self-conscious writing about animals as people?

Getting to know your main character

How old should your character be? As a children's writer, you'll undoubtedly wind up creating stories for different readership age levels. For this first writing exercise, just think of the age level where you feel most at home, but don't miss chapter two, with more on this topic.

Consider not only the children you're in contact with now in your every day life, but dig deep to dredge up your own childhood memories. Do you remember what it was like to be a six-year-old? What kinds of stories did you enjoy when you were six? Perhaps you find it easier to imagine yourself under the skin of a venturesome 11-year-old—or a shy one. Or maybe your teenage memories are the most vivid in your mind. As you contemplate ideas for this first story, let that sense of kinship be your guide.

To pursue this point a step further: in children's fiction, the age of a story's main character almost always determines its readership level. A rule of thumb is that kids want to read about characters their own age (at minimum) but usually a bit older. Therefore the 11-year-old mentioned above would be a suitable main character for readers in the eight-12, or middle-grade, range. A six-year-old main character wouldn't hold their interest, no matter how bright or appealing. Instead, save that character for readers or listeners in the four-to-seven age group. For teenaged readers, a main character, or protagonist (the terms are interchangeable), is usually at least 14 or 15.

Uh-oh

Make trouble for your main character. It may surprise you that I'm asking you to get your main character in trouble. But as you'll realize when you stop to think about it, every good story is built around a problem—a conflict or challenge for its protagonist.

If 10-year-old Adam wants a skateboard for Christmas and the skateboard duly appears under the tree on Christmas morning, do you have a story? No, because Adam hasn't had to do anything to achieve his wish. Suppose, though, that Adam's parents are opposed to skateboards, considering them dangerous. Somehow Adam must prove he can handle one safely. Practicing may be a problem, though. Now that his best buddy has moved away, the only skateboard in the neighborhood belongs to a girl he detests (and the feeling is mutual). *Now* you're on your way to a real story, thanks to the trouble you've created for Adam: the challenge, the obstacles. The reader will root for him, agonize over his setbacks, and rejoice in his eventual triumph. As you mull over ideas for your first story, remember that while it's nice in real life when things go smoothly, that just won't do for fiction. One way or another, your main character needs to *earn* that happy ending.

Putting Your Ideas into Words

Possibly you've been scribbling some notes as you read this section and looked back at your chosen picture—these are the informal jottings most writers make before they start work on a story. That's fine, but don't prolong the process. As you gain experience, you'll learn how much advance planning is right for you. For this first assignment, I'd like you to move right ahead into the writing of your story as soon as you're comfortable with your choice of main character and situation.

The words may not come easily at first, but don't be discouraged by a few dry runs. You may find that while the opening section unfolds easily, you're not sure just where your story is heading. In that case, go to a different section of whatever you're using to write on (that is, take another sheet of paper or scroll down your screen), write an ending you like, and then think backwards from there. (Incidentally, jokes are often created this way. The comedian hits on a punch line, then works on a story that will lead up to it. Detective stories, too, are frequently written backwards, the ingenious solution to a crime being clear in the writer's mind long before he or she has thought up the crime itself.)

As you work, don't try for a perfectly written story the first time through. Think of yourself as an artist with a sketch pad, jotting down a detail here, balancing it with another there, noting the main elements to be included in the finished painting. The important thing at this stage is just to get your ideas down. Then you can play with them, rearranging them if necessary so that your story develops logically from start to finish. Think of it as having three parts:

1. A beginning that introduces your main character in action and sets up a story problem

2. A middle that shows your character tackling the problem

3. An ending that resolves the problem

If you're working closely with your chosen picture, bear in mind that the event suggested by the picture doesn't necessarily have to occupy the body of your story. It's just a *prompt*. Literally, just a nudge to get you going. Your tale could concern events leading up to that particular moment so that it becomes the dramatic high point—the climax—of the story. Or the pictured scene could take place at the very start. Then the body of your story would deal with the consequences of that event, building to another dramatic moment as your protagonist struggles to meet the challenge you've concocted for him or her.

As we said earlier, you're also free to depart entirely from the pictured scene, possibly borrowing a detail or two from the image for inspiration—a setting, a character, an action. If you decide to strike out on your own, just remember to think "drama" as you write, so that your story will create its own vivid pictures in the reader's mind. Don't inhibit yourself right now by writing to a word count—you don't want to check your flow of ideas.

Fill in Details and Dialogue

Now you have your story roughly laid out, with events in an order that satisfies you. Now go back to the beginning and work in secondary details. Add a few descriptive words so that the reader will be able to visualize your characters. Do the same with your setting—the time and place of your story.

Dialogue as a key story element.

Your reader will want to hear your characters as well as see them, so get them talking! When you read the best books for children at your local indie bookstore, you will notice the major role played by dialogue—conversations between characters—in stories for young readers. Not only will dialogue bring your characters to life, it will also help move your story forward quickly and entertainingly.

Who Is Telling Your Story?

Earlier you read of the importance of identifying with your main character as you write. That identification is something you want your readers to feel as well, to the point where the events of your story will almost seem to be happening to them. (Think of the last story or novel you couldn't put down. Chances are your absorption stemmed from identification with a protagonist whose life you felt you were living as you read.)

The surest way to create this strong sense of identification in a young reader is to tell your story from your main character's point of view, and that point of view only, as if you were literally standing in his or her shoes. You (and therefore your reader) will have direct access to that character's thoughts, feelings, and sensations. If a cold rain is falling, your hero will feel it on his or her skin—and so will the reader. If your hero is impatient or puzzled—or sad or angry or happy—your reader will feel those emotions, too. In a sense the reader will become your hero.

The other characters in your story, of course, will have their own thoughts, sensations, and emotions—but you won't give these to the reader directly. Instead, you'll convey them through what your main character observes or infers: "Adam shrank from the look of fury in Jennie's eyes." If you were to move into Jennie's mind during this scene—"Jennie didn't think she'd ever been so mad"—you'd interrupt and perhaps destroy the reader's vital bonding with Adam as your main character.

Read Your Story Aloud

When you've finished going over your story a second time, read it out loud. Does it flow easily? Do the words and phrases feel comfortable in your mouth? Do they sound natural and pleasing to the ear? Whether yours is a read-aloud story for small children or a story for teenagers, your writing should be able to stand up to this test; even silent readers "hear" what they read with their inner ears.

Don't be too concerned about vocabulary at this stage, even if you're writing for the youngest age group. In the case of a read-aloud story, you should know that a child's listening vocabulary is far greater than what he or she can actually read at an early age. On the other hand, if you'd like your story to be readable by six- or seven-year-olds on their own, you'll want to keep your language simple and basic, with short (one- or two-syllable) words predominating. Actual word choice is important, of course, but you'll be refining your skill in that area later on.

Editing Your Story

You're into the home stretch now—and it's time to consider that word count. Have you ever heard the term "kill your darlings"? It means cut, cut, cut! It's hard to write. That's why it's so much harder to edit out what was so difficult to get down on the page. But every word must be there for a reason.

Look first for any extra detail: you may love it, and you may think it adds to your story, but ask yourself if it's really needed to move the action along. Pay special attention to your setting. As noted, you need to supply a sense of place, but you don't want to let descriptive details overwhelm or clutter your story, especially if you're writing a very young picture book. Apply the same test to dialogue, making sure it contributes to the story in some way—helping characterize, supplying necessary background information, or moving the plot forward.

Watch, too, for unnecessary "stage business." If Adam has a conversation on the school bus with his friend Ron, you don't need to preface that scene by describing how Adam climbed onto the bus, looked around for Ron, and made his way up the aisle to take the seat next to him. These are actions your readers will automatically supply for themselves.

Finally, check your phrases: Can you use a one-word synonym to replace three or four words? (This is where your thesaurus will come in handy.) For example, "Josh walked over to the gate with slow, lazy steps" might become "Josh ambled to the gate."

Again, cutting is usually a painful job for a writer, even for an experienced professional. There's a tendency to fall in love with your own words, and it hurts to discard favorite phrases, to say nothing of whole sentences or paragraphs. But the fact is that most writing is improved by cutting—and the chances are that yours will be too.

Note from Katie Davis: A very good editor at Harcourt once gave me the best writing advice I ever got, and it had to do with editing. I've taken this advice and used it on every book I've written and hope it will help you in your writing, too.

Once you've finished working on a manuscript, whether it's a light picture book, or heavy young adult novel, put it away for awhile. Once you've had some distance from the work, take it out and print it. Set aside a solid chunk of time to read it, and edit the story, writing on your printout. Once you've done that, sit down at your desk, and start a new document, using your marked up copy as your guide.

Yes, you're going to re-key in the entire manuscript. New things will blossom where you never expected them to, and the marks you made on your hard copy will give you ideas you didn't know you had.

4 _____

PLOTTING A GREAT STORY

Contributed by former Institute of Children's Literature instructor, Kathryn Jensen Johnson

The editor of a collection of holiday short stories gave only one stipulation to hopeful writers: Whatever you write must have something to do with Valentine's Day. Since the target age of my readers would be 10 to 14 years old, I also knew that my characters had to be teenagers. A third factor was my own mood: I felt like plotting something lighthearted and funny, perhaps slightly bittersweet—but nothing too heavy, since I'd just finished working on a serious problem novel. I needed a change of pace.

I began by thinking about a character and how he or she might be affected by the holiday. Maybe make the main character a boy who wants to spend Valentine's Day with his girlfriend. A simple wish, if the girl lives next door—or even across town. But since a story needs difficulties and complications, I decided the girlfriend would have moved to another state with her family. Nonetheless, the boy plans to surprise his love by showing up on Valentine's Day, loaded down with romantic gifts.

Who might this boy be? Because his being in a band would appeal to my teenage readers, I chose to make him a young musician. And since musicians just getting a start in the business are paid very little, he'd need to work hard to save up travel expenses. He'd also have to be a determined, spunky kid to cope with all of the things that might—and would—go wrong with his scheme.

The Planning Begins

Quickly I jotted down my list of snags, visualizing each event as a brief, dramatized scene. The boy would plan to fly, then realize how expensive plane fare was. The train would also be beyond his means. He'd opt for taking the bus, only to get stranded in a grimy bus depot. He'd run out of cash before he could purchase the romantic gifts. At last he'd arrive at his girlfriend's house to find she'd already started dating someone else and had very little interest in spending a romantic evening with him. Sigh!

But a Valentine's Day story should certainly have a happy ending. Perhaps I could reward my poor, disillusioned hero in an unexpected way? I imagined him making a new friend and, coincidentally, discovering a talented female singer for his band. Quickly I added these thoughts to my other notes.

When I reached this point in my planning, I'd completed a process every professional writer learns to go through before plunging into a first draft: the basic plotting of my story. I might make many changes before I was through writing and revising, but I'd already come up with a strong beginning, middle, and end for my story. I knew where my story would start (the boy's longing for his girlfriend, his Valentine's Day plan), how it would continue (the obstacles he'd have to face and overcome), and how it would end (the new friend, the new girl). Any details I changed or added along the way would remain within the basic framework I'd established.

What Exactly Is a Plot?

As you might have guessed, I love plotting. I adore experimenting with endless possibilities, fitting pieces together, making scenes work. In a sense, a plot mirrors life itself, with its pattern of birth, growth, and death. But a plot is really nothing more mysterious than a plan for a story—a sequence of events with a beginning, a middle, and an end.

The direction a plot takes may be simple and straightforward, as in a short story for preschoolers. Or it may be complex and twisting, with many complications, when intended for young adult readers. If I'm working on a book, it may include side plots along the way. But whether simple or complex, a strong plot grows from some kind of conflict or challenge the main character faces and acts upon.

A "slice of life" isn't enough. If I'd settled for placing my lovelorn teenage hero at a band rehearsal or performance and having him think about how much he misses his distant girlfriend, I might have had the makings of an interesting scene with some authentic musical detail, but I wouldn't have had a plot. Conflict and action are necessary elements; without them there is no story.

How the conflict is resolved will depend partly on the age of your intended reader. Most stories for small children end simply and happily. For older readers, the ending of a story will resolve the central conflict, giving a satisfying sense of completion, but may leave other questions open. My teenage musician, for example, will still have to struggle to keep his band afloat, and while there's a hint of new romance, there's no certainty that its path will run smoothly.

Whatever the story's resolution, though, a good plot will enforce some kind of positive change or growth on the main character. A kindergarten child who misplaces his lunch and then must find it before noon or go hungry learns to use simple deductive reasoning to locate his missing meal. He will also learn to take responsibility for his belongings in the future. Similarly, my musical hero realizes that people's feelings can change, including his own, and that as one door closes, another may open. It's this character growth that gives a story its meaning, or theme.

Taking Control of Your Story

Planning and organizing a whole story in your head or on paper may seem like a lot of unnecessary bother. I've been told by some new writers that it's easier for them simply to start writing with a few characters in mind, then let these paper people take the story where they will. Isn't that a far more creative way of storytelling?

Unfortunately, without some forethought on the part of the author, plots tend to play naughty tricks. They wander, wind up at dead ends, become vague and confusing, and fail to resolve themselves satisfactorily. Young readers—and the editors who serve them—are especially quick to sense this lack of control. They know when a writer has lost his or her way and is grasping at plotting straws. They stop believing in the story, put it down unfinished, and return to their TVs and video games (or to other manuscripts, in the case of editors).

I once wrote a story about a young ballet dancer. Because I'd taken ballet as a child and still dearly love classical dance, I was determined to add plenty of realistic details. I just started writing, riding my joy for the words I was creating and my enthusiasm for the topic. I ended up with a non-story that was three times too long for the market I'd targeted. While I was filling up pages with lovely ballet terms, I was searching for a plot that never fully came to be. I had no conflict. I hadn't done my planning.

Conversely, young readers will sense when a writer has a definite game strategy. They trust the story will progress in a logical pattern and will arrive at a logical (but not too easily predicted) conclusion. In a sense, we as authors sign a pact with our readers: They'll go on reading because they trust us to play fair with them and deliver what we've promised.

Create a Road Map

Not only does outlining my plot help me maintain control over what happens in my story, it also helps me control its length—often a vital matter in writing for young readers. For example, a typical magazine length for middle-grade stories is 1,200 words. Since I type an average of 250 words per page, using double spacing, that means my manuscript can be no more than five pages long.

Visualizing that limited space will affect the way I plot my story. I can see right away that it will need to get off to a fast start, introducing my main character and conflict as quickly as possible. The middle of my story can probably accommodate no more than two or three separate scenes. And certainly there won't be space to dawdle over my ending! (This doesn't mean, by the way, that such a plot has to be a simple one. As we gain experience as writers, we discover ways of compressing and telescoping events in order to leave room for those two or three crucial storytelling scenes.)

Yes, there are a few published writers who declare to interviewers that they never work from outlines and simply let the writing flow. I believe this is rarely a successful method. Most authors I know outline in detail before they begin writing. Jotting down even a brief overview of your story gives you a valuable tool and won't detract from the excitement of actually writing the scenes. I don't use dialogue at all in my outlines for just this reason. And I always use present tense in my plotting notes, so that when I shift to past tense for my story, the prose will feel fresh and new to me.

Simply put, plotting gives a writer a much better chance of completing a publishable story.

Old Stories into New

New writers often worry unnecessarily about originality. The truth is, conjuring up a totally original plot is impossible even for an experienced writer. Willa Cather, the famed novelist of the early twentieth century, wrote, "There are only two or three human stories, and they go on repeating themselves as fiercely as if they had never happened before."

Even if the total count of major plots is as high as five or six, a writer who racks his or her brains in search of the one fantastic plot that everyone else has missed is barking up the wrong tree. What such a writer needs to understand is that the strength and distinctiveness of a good plot develop from a blend of story elements a particular writer pulls together, then strains through his or her own experiences and view of the world.

One story I wrote for young adult readers featured a handsome prince, a young, overworked woman who was a commoner, a grand ball at a glamorous castle, and a happily-ever-after wedding. Sound familiar? It's the Cinderella story, of course. But because it was set in today's world, not in the fairy-tale past, and because the heroine was a typical modern girl any teenager could identify with, it came across freshly enough to intrigue my readers.

This isn't to suggest a writer can or should throw creativity to the wind. Experienced writers learn that although they can't hope to deliver a plot unlike any other, they can and should experiment with stories that include unusual twists—something special that intrigues, surprises, or even shocks. What that something is depends upon the characters, conflict, setting, time frame, and other specific details chosen by the author, as well as upon the author's personal writing style or "voice."

And a related point: some people claim that good science fiction, sports, mystery, and romantic stories can be written according to specific formulas. This is not true. If it were, computers would be churning out books and human writers like you and me would be out of a job. Although some elements are similar in each of these genres, copycat writing is always detectable. It rings false, is riddled with clichés, and lacks an authentic voice.

The Birth of a Plot

For most writers, the germ of a story plot is a single, simple idea that starts things rolling. It may come from a personal experience, an incident related by a friend, a person (either real or imaginary), a TV news item, or an intriguing fact glimpsed in a travel guide. Ideas are limitless, and they can't be copyrighted. They hang in the air all around us, just waiting for us to pluck them like ripe fruit from a bountiful tree.

Here are some sources of inspiration students have shared with me in talking about their stories:

"One of my elderly aunts has recounted her terror as a child, living through the bombing of London during World War II."

"The idea for a novel set during the Depression came to me from my father-in-law's real experiences."

"A summer trip to a state park inspired my picture book idea."

"Having coached Little League baseball for many years, I have witnessed the ways children can be cruel. I wanted to show them how to be fair to teammates who may seem different."

My own fiction has come from such diverse sources as fascination with certain historical periods (the Vietnam War era, the War of 1812), a dream about dinosaurs running loose in Yellowstone Park (for a picture book), meeting a teenager who worked summers on a cruise ship, and the receipt of a mysterious fan letter. I also wrote a novel called *Crash Course* that was inspired by a personal fear—that of drowning.

Character as a Starting Point

For many children's writers, a story plot may begin with an imagined main character rather than with an external idea. In a case like that, I try to generate a problem situation for the child or teenager, drawing on elements of that character's invented biography. Then I add a degree of internal conflict based on the character's personality traits.

One of my stories featured a teenage girl who, despite a family rule, planned on giving a Halloween party while her parents were out of town. Although she was basically a good kid, her stubbornness and her desire to please her friends got her into serious trouble when an uninvited guest spiked the punch, endangering the heroine's younger brother when he sampled it.

An advantage of using a character as your starting point is the natural lead-in to meaningful plot development—events in which your protagonist not only takes an active part but that concern him or her vitally. But whatever the source of

48

your plot idea, it's important to decide at the outset why the outcome will matter to your main character. If he or she won't be directly affected by the story conflict or has no more than a small stake in how things work out, the reader will have little reason to care what happens. This aspect of plotting has to do with motivation, something that needs to be firmly in place before you begin detailing your story events.

Basic Human Needs as a Starting Point

For my own purposes, I divide all plots into three motivational categories: survival, love, and achievement. These three incentives from real life provide all the drama and emotion any story needs. Think for a moment about one of your favorite stories; I guarantee it is based on one or more of these categories.

Survival is the instinctive drive of all living creatures to prolong life in the face of physical or emotional adversity. We need food, shelter, companionship, and our health to survive. Love includes love of family, of objects, loyalty to friends and mate. The desire for achievement can be healthy when sought for personal growth through education or to better an individual's living conditions. But it is destructive when greed takes over and results in harm to others—war and murder being the ultimate evil forms of achievement.

If I'm stuck on how to move from a character into a plot actively involving him or her, I always think about these three basic human needs: survival, love, and achievement.

Tailoring Plot to Your Readers

Another important consideration as you begin laying out your plot is the readership age for which your story material is suited. Consider the following plot germs: a near-drowning experience, a trip to visit a girlfriend, vivid remembrances of a war. Chances are you'll see immediately that these are appropriate subjects for older readers—12 years and up. Each deals with a situation that a beginning or even middle-grade reader would find confusing or troubling. On the other hand, if a tale concerns a family trip to Maine, a classroom drawing contest, or a 10-year-old's experiences growing up on a farm during the American Civil War, you'll be gearing your plot to a younger audience.

Remember that children want to read about characters their own age or a few years older. I always try to develop a plot that will encourage young readers to identify strongly with the main character, so that they feel they have a stake in seeing the conflict resolved happily.

I also constantly remind myself that my plot must have sufficient interest and entertainment value for the age level I've targeted.

One of my novels for teenage readers came about through another dance love—ballroom dancing. I wanted to convey the excitement and dedication needed to perform with a partner to beautiful music.

But I knew that teenagers need lots of action and emotional tension in their stories, and they like surprises. Just telling the story of a young dancer whose goal is to win a major competition wouldn't produce a plot complex enough to sustain a 200-page manuscript. What to do?

Dying to Dance ended up as a murder mystery, with the heroine suspected of doing away with her chief competitor. I added a gentle love interest, so that when the heroine becomes a suspect, she risks losing her career, her freedom . . . and her new boyfriend. (To my teenage readers, this third loss may have seemed the most important of all!) The basic situation was nothing new—many mystery plots center on rivalry as a motive for crime—but setting the story in the world of competitive dancing gave it freshness, made it fun for my teen readers, and allowed me to include some unusual plot twists. At the same time, the story was able to convey a clear message about the dangers of taking competitiveness too far.

At the other extreme in terms of length and readership age is the very first piece of fiction I ever published—the read-aloud story for preschoolers I mentioned earlier, about the little boy who misplaced his lunch. I wanted to write a mystery story that even a very young child could enjoy and participate in. For this one, I used a simple, linear plot, no twists or turns. The boy thinks about all the places he has been during the morning in school. Finally he realizes that the last time he saw his lunch sack, he was on the bus. And that's where he finds it . . . in the nick of time to share his noon meal with his classmates.

Charting a Course: The Beginning

Once I've chosen a main character, settled on a definite story situation, and given my character a meaningful conflict to resolve, I'll have plotted the beginning of my story, even if I'm not yet sure just what my opening paragraphs will contain.

Now I should be ready to start brainstorming the incidents, twists, and turns that will make up my story's middle (and longest) section . . . shouldn't I?

Yes—if I know how my story will end. But sometimes that can be a big "if" for a writer. It's tempting to tell myself I'll decide on the ending later, after I've got most of my story down on paper. Usually that's a mistake. In order to chart a logical course, I need to have a clear idea of my destination.

When writing mysteries, for example, I plan the beginning

scenes, then think about how I want the story to end. Only when I know that (whodunit and why the crime took place) can I build a logical plot, playing fair with my readers but also playfully misleading them by scattering confusing clues along the way. If I don't know where I'm headed, I risk writing myself into a corner or deciding at the last minute on a solution to the mystery that doesn't make sense and may require a great deal of rewriting to support it.

The same thing applies to plotting other kinds of stories. I may know vaguely that I want things to end happily, with the immediate conflict resolved to everyone's satisfaction. But how is this to be accomplished? Now's the time to decide, so that all of my plot events feed into that solution. Equally important, I need to visualize a degree of inner growth and change for my main character. Will he or she be a slightly different person at the end of the story? If not, I may be plotting a "So what?" narrative rather than a meaningful story.

Into the Thick of Things: The Middle

Once I begin plotting the middle of my story, I'm dealing with cause and effect—with actions and reactions. If this occurs, what happens as a result? When Josie, my teenage heroine in the novel *Pocket Change*, follows her father out of the house one night, she discovers he's not fully awake. He's lost in a war that ended before she was born, and he's a very troubled man. Knowing this, she must decide what she can and should do to help her father . . . even if he refuses her help and denies he has a problem. His actions create a reaction from her. Then her actions create new reactions from him. This dramatic pattern continues until the final scene of the story.

As I work with cause and effect, I try to keep logic and plausibility in mind. A character who has always behaved cautiously and is not physically strong won't be likely to take sudden risks or perform dangerous feats of agility unless she's highly motivated and has somehow prepared herself to handle the task. A science fiction story that features technologically advanced citizens will not be believable if the conflict is resolved by a child who pushes the right button on a control panel after all the brilliant scientists have forgotten such a button exists. In mysteries, it's unlikely a child will be capable of figuring out a complex crime if trained police officers fail miserably.

I constantly ask myself if the actions portrayed in my scenes make sense. If my honest answer is, "Not really, but I need this to happen for the story to work," then I know I must find another way to make my plot happen.

The Big Moment . . . and Then the Ending

As I rough out a plot, I think of its events as building toward a single dramatic moment, much the way storm clouds gather in the sky, collecting moisture from the air, gathering force, finally exploding with a downpour and lightning crashing all around. In most stories, this will be the moment when my main character takes decisive action to resolve his or her problem—both the external problem (reaching an out-of-state girlfriend) and the internal conflict that has complicated his or her struggle (misunderstanding their relationship).

This is the story's climax scene, a moment of maximum tension for both protagonist and reader—a moment that finally gives way to release and resolution. While I may not know just how I'll handle that big scene until I get into the actual writing of my story, its basic content needs to be firmly in place as the cornerstone of my plot.

Once the main conflict has been resolved, I've arrived at

my story's denouement (a term you may remember from high school English class), the wrap-up of events that follows the climax scene. Ordinarily this will be very brief, a matter of a few sentences, and doesn't need to be included in a plot plan. The exception is a long story or book where the reader will need time to decompress after the emotion-filled climax scene and where the author may also need to tie up subplots and other loose ends before releasing the reader.

The Payoff

Is all this planning worth the effort? Yes, yes, yes! Thoughtful plotting results in strong, believable stories with the best chance of publication. And the process can be exhilarating, too. As I planned each exciting scene in my plot for "Duet," the Valentine's Day story mentioned earlier, I felt almost as if I were riding a rollercoaster with my hero.

Though I went on to make a number of changes during the writing process—including adding a troublesome guitarist and reshaping the girlfriend into the band's former singer, thus doubling her loss to the hero—my initial plotting gave my idea the form and shape it needed for development into a successful story. Avon Flare's editor agreed. "Duet" was published less than a year later in a short story collection called *Be Mine* . . . along with three other authors' romantic stories that had been just as carefully plotted.

What Kind of Story Are You Writing?

As you begin shaping your story idea into a plot, keep an eye on the end product. Is yours to be an adventure story? A sports story? A mystery? Humor? Fantasy?

Thinking in terms of story categories can guide you to likely markets for your manuscripts. Fiction editors have definite needs, whether they're putting together a magazine issue or choosing titles for a book publisher's semi-annual list. These needs are mentioned in their market listings. ("Stories of cultural diversity are always welcome here." "We're looking for strong historical fiction.")

Here's a rundown of fiction categories for which there's an ongoing demand in the children's market. Of course, many stories and novels combine elements of several types—a teen sports story may also contain a romance, for example, just as a humorous tale for beginning readers may address a real-life problem.

- Real-life fiction. Contemporary characters coping with problems, from everyday concerns to serious moral and social issues.

- Multicultural fiction. Ranges from contemporary stories with ethnic elements to folktales and stories set in other lands.

- Adventure. A quest, a flight, a challenge—and plenty of obstacles along the way. The emphasis is on fast-paced action.

- Sports. What it takes to win, what it means to lose— in the context of a specific sport, specifically presented.

- Mystery and suspense. Puzzle-solving in all its forms, from small backyard mysteries to real-world crime— though without depictions of actual violence except at the older-teen level.

- Romance. Classic plots using authentic details of today's teen culture, and often bittersweet rather than happy endings.

- Humor. Amusing characters and situations, quirky plot twists, neat resolutions. Humor that builds—no jokes or one-liners.

- Fantasy and science fiction. Instant make-believe for youngest readers, invented worlds—whether past, future, or extraterrestrial—for middle-graders and adolescents.

- Historical fiction. Believable characters, a good story, and imaginative research can bring even the most distant time and place alive.

- Animal stories. A beloved genre that's been updated to stress documented animal behavior and habitats. Animals-as-humans remain fine story characters for young children; for older readers, realism in depicting animals is a must.

Staying on Course

Here are some points that help me as I plot a story toward its climax. They may help you, too.

- Coincidences weaken a story. If two young girls move to the same school from out of state, how likely will it be for them to discover they are long-lost twin sisters? It could happen, but will the reader believe this? What about a boy who, having fallen down a deep hole, finds one end of a rope at the bottom that's been securely tied to a tree above? Editors are leery of plotting devices that stretch the reader's faith too far. Ask yourself: What are the chances of this really happening?

- Keeping your cast of characters small will help your plot stay focused. Even in a 10-to-14 or young adult short story, you probably don't need more than four or five characters.

- Adult characters should keep a low profile. Kids want to read about other kids coping with problems and challenges, whether these involve facing down the closet monster at bedtime or winning a place on the high school swim team. If your conflict can only be resolved by helpful adults, you need to rethink your plot.

- A narrow time frame is a boon to tight, suspenseful plotting. Most stories for young readers take place over a few weeks at most, and many occur within a period of a few hours. If yours will need to deal with an important event that happened prior to the main action, you have several options. Your characters can refer to that event in dialogue; your main character can relive it in a memory flash; or you can dip into the past by means of a flashback—a fully dramatized scene. Since this last choice will interrupt the "now" time of your story and can be confusing to a child reader, it's best reserved for fiction intended for teens and young adults.

- The scenes you plot should allow for variety of pace and intensity. A story can't be a series of high-emotion peaks or action scenes, not only because the reader needs time to recover, but also because events need to build to a clear climax at the story's end. On the other hand, a story that includes no dramatic scenes throughout the beginning and middle but concludes with a slam-bang chase scene will lack conviction because of poor pacing.

- Varying your settings will add interest and momentum. Even a simple story for youngest readers will feel sluggish if it takes place in just one room. If you move the characters from school to home, then out to the backyard, the plot will seem more active.

Ten-Point Plotting Checklist

Just as pilots run an equipment check before takeoff, you can check the effectiveness of your plot before launching the story toward a publisher.

Does your story have:

- a main character actively and emotionally involved in resolving a conflict?

- a conflict important enough to hold the reader's interest? Is it introduced early?

- age-appropriate features, including suitable length, characters, and situation?

- sufficient motivation for the protagonist? Is it clear why the outcome of this story is important to the main character?

- several varied scenes that provide forward plot motion?

- a logical basis for characters' behavior, as well as a natural cause-and-effect sequence of events?

- a unified plot that does not wander into unrelated territory?

- chronology that will be easily followed by the reader?

- a believable and satisfying climax brought about by the main character?

- all crucial loose ends tied up by the end, including those introduced in secondary plots?

5 _____

WHAT EDITORS WISH
WRITERS KNEW

Below is the transcript of a chat with an editor of a major publishing company, hosted and moderated by Jan Fields. The attendees are Institute of Children's Literature students. Because they're our students they have access to perks like this fantastic educational event.

Jan: WELCOME to GUEST SPEAKER CHAT with our mystery children's book editor. I'm your host, moderator, and resident pontificator— Jan Fields. I'm looking forward to learning a lot about the things editors wish all of us writers knew, and would do. Welcome Editor of Mystery and thanks for joining us tonight!

Mystery editor: Thank you, Jan. Happy to be here.

Jan: Yes, and you look lovely typing away with the bag over your head, Mystery editor.

Mystery editor: Yes, it's a lovely designer bag.

Jan: Only the best for the editors. Now, into the fray!

WritingMadly: Could you make a 'Top Ten List of Do's and Don'ts' in terms of getting published/slush pile?

Mystery editor: Hoo-boy. Well, the first thing you do is accept that writing for children is a profession. And like any profession, there is a learning period. There are writers who say, "I don't want to be a professional writer, I just have this idea." Screeeee! Writing for children is not like writing for other genres. Just like anything else, you LEARN the profession before you begin practicing it. The slush pile is FULL of stories people jotted down on a whim without learning one iota about the biz.

Mystery editor: Learn what makes a good children's story. Read CURRENT (last five years) books in your chosen genre—— picture books, middle grade, etc. Read AWARD winners. There are critique groups, conferences, the SCBWI, message boards, tons and tons and TONS of info out there for you.

So what you DO is 1. Constantly work on improving your craft. 2. Read, read, read. 3. Write, write, write. 4. Study the markets, carefully target.

Common Writing Flaws or How to Stay in Slush Forever

1. Bad rhyme, weak, inconsistent, or non-existent meter. Reading that is like listening to a tone deaf person sing. After the first bar (line), you are ready to run.

2. Picture books over 1,000 words. 600-800 or less is pretty good. Single spacing, weird fonts, not putting the word count down are not effective methods of disguising a too-long picture book. I can tell in a glance if it's too many words ... and there's always the heft of too many pages.

3. Stories with obvious knock-you-over-the-head morals. Don't even put the words moral, lesson, teach, value, or anything of that ilk in your cover letter. It sends off sirens and flashing lights in the editor's head.

4. If you are writing a contemporary story, use contemporary names. A story set in 1975 is NOT contemporary. Donald, Billy, Penny, Brandy, Misty, are NOT contemporary names. It's okay to have one or two of those ... but quick go find me a fourth grade classroom TODAY with a Hugh, Dennis, Sharon, Craig, Susan, AND Nancy in it all at the same time. You aren't going to find one.

5. While I'm on the subject of names, watch the alliteration. If you are choosing alliterative names, choose something that matches the character ... just don't choose the name based on the alphabet. Sizzle the Snake instead of Sammy Snake. But again ... go easy ... don't make EVERY single character name in your story alliterative. By the time the editor gets to her third Timmy Turtle of the day, she wants to hurt somebody.

6. FOLLOW DIRECTIONS on submission guidelines. Don't think you know a better way. You do not know how the office works or the personal work preferences of the acquiring editor. Guidelines are set up for the editor/publisher's convenience.

7. Every story needs a beginning, a middle, and an end. It also needs plot, conflict, and setting. Oh yeah ... and characters.

8. Follow proper manuscript format. Double space. Use one side of the paper. Use black ink.

9. For picture books do not include amateur illustrations. For some reason, people like to do their own computer-generated illustrations. Don't include illustration notes unless they are ESSENTIAL to the story, i.e., something vital to the story has to be communicated in the pictures. Don't put something like: Grandmother is wearing a pink dress with lace around the collar and she is holding a blue cup as she walks past her slightly wilting petunias. Don't include page breaks.

10. Don't be boring. You don't have time to let the story warm up. You need to grab the editor with the first sentence, and not let them go. You truly only have a few seconds to get the editor's attention.

Jan: I saw that you mention long picture books, what do you think is the optimal picture book length these days for most publishers?

Mystery editor: 500ish words. 600 maybe, definitely aim for under 800. You can get by with slightly over 1,000, but much over ... is really stretching it.

Jan: And if you have a long picture book, you have to do a lot of extra market research to find the publishers doing those—I know Peachtree has done a couple at 1,200 words. DON'T just send it to all the picture book publishers on the assumption that they will publish a 1,000+ text if it's good enough— they won't. Not if they only run shorter ones. You have to study their books.

Mystery editor: Correct. I'm sure they exist. But what I see a lot of in slush is really old-fashioned, moralistic tales that go on and on. Those just aren't in vogue any more. There is a thing called a picture story book, but they are rare.

Jan: Now, I know some of the things folks send you as picture books really need to be something else, even when they're good— do you find that? Stuff that ought to be, say, a magazine story, or maybe expanded into a chapter book, but not a picture book?

Mystery editor: Yes, I see that a lot. I see a lot of things that would really make good magazine stories. They are good stories, but they don't have that "read me over and over again" quality, and they don't have enough illustration possibilities. They don't change scenes often enough. Others could be expanded into chapter books, so I see a lot of things that are good that aren't really picture books, at least not what the market will support today.

froggy: Do you find more of a need for a particular age group?

Mystery editor: I think that depends by house and what the focus is. At my own house it can vary. If we have enough of one thing we may begin zeroing in on another area. Watch the house you are interested in and see what they are putting the most out of each year/season.

SamIam: As an editor do you see many series books submitted?

Mystery editor: Yes, I do, and those are kinda iffy from unknowns. Usually you want to see how one book will do before you take on a series. Usually you will want to send one as a "stand alone" and don't mention the series potential until you are farther along in the acquisition process.

chuffchuff: Can your 8-12 novel be read without agent representation?

Mystery editor: Of course it can, if you send it to an open house or one still accepting unsolicited queries.

snowman: What do editors look for in a picture book biography?

Mystery editor: My house does few of those. You do want it to be different from what else is on the market. If your subject is common or well known, do research to make sure you have a different angle. Do a market survey and have the info available on how yours is different from what else is there.

SeeSawboy: I know this is probably impossible to get an answer but how do you ever know if your writing is any good if no one ever has time to jot down a few comments? It would be nice to know if we are truly wasting everyone's time if it isn't worthy of publication.

Mystery editor: That business of "is my writing any good" is really your responsibility. There are megatons of info on the internet and in books. There are critique groups. There are opportunities to get paid critiques at conferences. There are message boards and support groups and all kinds of things out there. Read, read, read, read, read, read. Go to Linda Sue Parks' web site. Do what she did. Read, read, read, read. With enough experience and knowledge you KNOW the difference between great, good, average, and oh, never mind. Do you really want a rejection that says, "This manuscript is awful. I'd say kill it, but it's already dead. Please be kind to the earth and recycle." No. Writers are tender creatures. And it's all one big learning curve. The clunky writer of today might be the best seller of tomorrow ... IF that person does his homework. And I guess this is a good time to bring this up ... it's subjective. I'm usually not going to put a reason in unless I think it will help.

JerBer: I know that as a writer of a picture book manuscript I'm not supposed to give any indication of what visuals I "see" for the story. I have a manuscript which I've written specifically about a mixed race child (black and white). This is something I feel quite strongly about, as my own family looks like this. It is a growing segment of our culture, and yet it's not reflected in children's literature. I wrote a page, in addition to the manuscript, in which I've described her world—the urban neighborhood and apartment where she lives in Brooklyn, her mother, father, grandmother, and best friends. Is it appropriate to send that background page along with the manuscript, or should I simply devote a couple of sentences to it in my query letter? Or, not say anything at all and let the manuscript stand on its own? (And hope, when it sells, that we'll be able to talk about these additional things.)

Mystery editor: I'd mention in the cover letter that it is a biracial child. If the exact setting is important then there should be indications of that in the manuscript. You can establish setting in a picture book without getting TOO descriptive. Just a thought, consider moving away from stereotypes. Biracial children live in all sorts of circumstances ... suburbs ... rural areas ... it's not just an inner city sorta thing. I'm getting that the MOST important thing here is that the child is seen as biracial— so I'd make that clear.

froggy: Do you look for proper English and grammar?

Mystery editor: Of course! However, one or two minor mistakes won't throw you out of the running if it's a good story. But, yes, you need to use the Queen's English properly. Demonstrate a command of the language. Competition is too stiff. An editor isn't really going to sign on to clean up poor writing even if the idea might be good underneath.

Jan: Plus, a nice clean manuscript with good spelling, and grammar and punctuation looks like you didn't rush it. Editors don't like the rushed vibes.

Mystery editor: Definitely. It looks like you know your stuff and you didn't just take up writing an hour ago.

Mystery editor: What I meant was don't stress if you realize after you sent a manuscript that you used "their" instead of "there." But you should strive for perfection. The exception would be in dialogue. You need to be true to your character's voice. But a manuscript riddled with mistakes and full of poor grammar is going to go back a.s.a.p.

Jan: Now, lady of mystery, I know one of the things you said you watch for in cover letters is whether a writer will be easy to deal with— so what kinds of things might make a person look difficult (so I can never ever do them)?

Mystery editor: I don't want to hear personal sob stories that are irrelevant to the writing, for example your employment status. Don't tell the editor what they will think. Don't bring up money or advance. Don't whine about the state of the publishing industry. Don't grovel and say things like, "I'll change anything you want." That shows me you don't believe in your own story.

Jan: The "I'll change anything you want" also suggests you don't understand the editorial process—of course you'll make some changes as the book goes through editing. But some things at the heart of the book you might want to hold fast to. Editors know that.

Mystery editor: Only list relevant accomplishments, and it really doesn't matter how much your children love your story.

- On cover letters—If you list published works, state with whom it was published. If you are ashamed to identify the whom, then don't mention the credit. Folks will wonder. If the name of the publisher shows up unfavorably, don't include the credit.

- Cover letters should be short, sweet, professional.

- Don't act difficult—bringing up money in the cover, acting arrogant. Not sure how I can explain that … some writers can come across as though they are royalty and the editor is the peasant.

- I'm not sure people realize how things come across. Be professional is the best I can say. And don't admit that you are unpublished. It doesn't matter. The story matters.

Jan: You don't have to make up publication credits if you're unpublished; just leave that part out—focus on the work.

Jan: How about things like "marketing plans" or "promotional plans" or the like. Some folks really feel like they need that, but I have trouble finding any editors who want to see it. Not at the submission stage anyway.

Mystery editor: Oooh … that's a gray area. Some publishers want that stuff, and they will say so in their guidelines. Other times it can come across too strong.

Mystery editor: Don't act like a used car salesman. Don't put on the hard sale and use a lot of, ummm … persuasive language. You aren't Joe down at the car lot. Be professional and genuine and show a bit of your own personality. But really, the story needs to do the talking.

chuffchuff: Will an agent and magazine credits help an unpublished author?

Mystery editor: Yes. Maybe. They are perks. Not absolutely vital, but they help. Magazine credits are most helpful if they are from well-known, respected magazines. Those credits show that you have learned to take editorial direction and you are writing publishable material. Eeek … I almost hate to say it but there are a lot of little publications that just don't have the quality ... but there are other ones that do.

dawnword: Does it influence you if the author has an MFA in writing?

Mystery editor: Nope, I don't care. I want to know if they can write, not if they've just been taught to write. It may help the writer in the long run, but it doesn't impress me. Folks with a high school education can often write as well or better.

froggy: Do editors of children's lit like stories based on real kids?

Mystery editor: Yes, I think so. Again, that's a per house thing. You need to study their list/catalogs see what their trends are. There are specific publishers who want that sort of thing.

Marta: What is the best way to get noticed in the children's book industry today? Sometimes, it seems that the children's book industry is over-saturated.

Mystery editor: It is over-saturated. There are more good, even great stories than will ever be published. There is always room for new fresh voices. The best way to get noticed ... have a professional attitude and write a ripping good story.

Marta: What stands out? What would make an editor take notice of a new writer? Is it reasonable to think that the odds are almost impossible to break into the children's writing industry?

Mystery editor: Strong, fresh writing with authentic voice stands out. That's how new writers get noticed. Competition is stiff, but the odds aren't impossible. If you are thinking of children's writing as a means to make a living or if publication is your primary goal, you probably need a Plan B.

Marta: Is there a special formula to get noticed as a children's book writer?

Mystery editor: Nope, if there were, I'd package it and patent it! Seriously, the "secrets" have all been discussed. Everything that I have acquired or taken to acquisitions has a common thread ... I fell in love immediately, instantly, head over heels. The story was different. It stood out from the pack. There wasn't another one like it. Something about the story touched ME. There was a connection somewhere ... somehow ... chemistry. It's this wonderful, giddy I-HAVE-TO-HAVE-that-one feeling.

froggy: How do you make the editor excited about your story?

colorpalette: What makes a query or a sub leap from the slush and have you jumping up and down in glee?

Mystery editor: You write an incredible story. It's a matching game. I'm not sure you can MAKE them excited. It happens if you get the incredible story to the right person.

Mystery editor: The story is different. Not an everyday ordinary story. Not one I've already seen a hundred times. And it's a personal connection. The thing about falling in love is true. I'm thinking of one that I'm taking to acquisitions now. It spoke to me on about four different levels. It was superb writing and it touched on things that mattered or struck a chord with me. Magic.

colorpalette: Should you send your first story to multiple editors?

frostyboy: Are simultaneous submissions a good way to send out stories?

Mystery editor: First story? As in the first story you've ever written. Usually, you should save the first story you've ever written as a souvenir. You need to run a "first" story by a knowledgeable critique group. Multiple editors? Carefully SELECTED multiple editors.

Mystery editor: Yes, simultaneous subs are good unless the house asks for exclusives. Sim subs make sense. It's the smart way to do it.

Jan: My first submission was a horror, and I'd been a professional writer for adults for YEARS ... it takes a lot of practice and study to really do something that can compete in today's market for kids. It's a wonder the editor didn't write rude things on my first one. She said something nice and vague about my "skills" I think.

Mystery editor: Yep, I don't mean to be crass, but first stories sent to multiple publishers is what causes slush pile terrors.

Stephen: What do you think publishing houses can do (i.e. change) to facilitate their acceptance of manuscripts, reading of same, and replying yes or no to writers within let's say 8 to 12 weeks maximum?

Mystery editor: That's a tall order, and honestly, writers can do a lot to solve that problem. 1. Carefully target your submissions. 2. Do not submit until you are writing professional-level quality. 80-90 percent of the manuscripts received are just not viable. If the slush pile were smaller, it would be quicker to go through it. Unfortunately, many publishers have to close their doors to unsolicited subs and rely on agented submissions. Agents serve as quality control. Reading slush is really like looking for the proverbial needle in the haystack.

Jan: I think a lot of publishers are trying to work on that problem— it's just that their solutions don't make writers happy because they usually focus on reducing the amount of slush— closing to unsolicited, closing to unagented, closing except to editors you meet at workshops and conferences, closing except for short times each year, closing except for contest entries once a year. All of that helps the problem, but the problem is being caused by the flood, not the publishers.

momo: Are ezines as credible for credits as print mags?

Mystery editor: They can be if they have a good reputation. It does show that you are actively writing. That you aren't a one-trick pony. That you understand the process. It may matter to some editors and not to others. Like the MFA question, it's nice, include it, but ultimately it's the story that matters.

Jan: For the most part, what I think ezines can do for you is (1) give you confidence in your writing— cause someone liked it, (2) let you dip your toes in the publishing process, and (3) have the fun of seeing your name on a story that other folks are reading .

Jan: But our mystery lady is not the first who's said really what they want to know is did you just send them something they love?

Mystery editor: Yes! I don't mean to discount other credits. They are good. They help you develop and grow as a writer. But when it comes down to "Do I want to buy this?" it doesn't make that big of an impact.

Frostyboy: Can you recommend a good resource book for grammar?

Jan: I just wanted to say here you can find some great grammar lesson things online ... and those in the audience who are <u>Institute of Children's Literature</u> students get the *Essentials of English* handbook which covers a lot— really, reading it is good.

Mystery editor: There are grammar books of all sorts available in book stores. A basic grammar book will be fine. There are also online sources. I think you have to find what works for you. Look through them.

Mystery editor: Some people like the silly ones, oh like that Vampire themed one ... *Transitive Vampire*? And there's the *Eat, Shoots and Leaves* one. I may have butchered the title. You don't have to be a stodgy grammarian, but having a good working knowledge puts you ahead of the game. You also have a better chance of getting good critique partners.

You can get a good grammar book from your library. Or maybe take a refresher course from your community center. My local YMCA offers grammar courses.

van27: If you can illustrate as well as write, should you?

sparton: What if you want to submit photographs for a story?

Mystery editor: Yes, if you are a professional illustrator or a professional photographer. If they are of professional quality, send together. It's another gray area. Or it might be best to just mention in the cover that photos are available. If you are an author/illustrator that can be a good thing.

sparton: Is there a certain theme in children's lit that is overdone?

Mystery editor: I think it comes in trends, but I see things that are stereotypical. Particularly the new kid moves in, bully, being popular school story. There are a lot of very sweet stories about babies and grandparents that just don't have enough story in them. They are very personal. Let me think what else ... Stories with the "Ugly Duckling" message or the "I want to be something else. No, I'll just learn to be myself."

sparton: Is it okay to re-submit a (revised) manuscript to an editor whose positive feedback you were given two years ago? I received an encouraging rejection letter on a picture book manuscript from an editor at Random House. She said she liked the voice but thought the book should be longer, like a chapter book or MG novel. So I rewrote it, and it's now a lower middle-grade novel. Sorry for the long question.

Mystery editor: It wouldn't bother me, and generally I think it would be okay because it's substantially different. If an editor gives you a personal comment on a rejection, it's usually not an invitation to resubmit unless they specifically say so. Two years later—sure, I'd go for it. Again—things vary. Editors have quirks.

Jan: One thing that freaks editors out is if they say, "This would make a nice novel," and a week later they get it as a very, very rough draft of a novel.

Jan: Never rush and lose the warm feeling the editor had about your potential.

Mystery editor: Oh, yes! And you also get reluctant to give personals, when people think, oh, comments, that means she wants to see it again.

Mystery editor: Don't send those revisions back TOO soon. Some people can revise quickly, but most of them can't. The revision is just not there yet, and then, whoops, you've blown your chance. You probably won't get a second revision request.

western: Do you like stories written in first person or third person?

Mystery editor: Either way if they are incredible stories. Whatsoever you doeth, doeth it expertly. Waiting for lightning strike.

Jan: **boom**

estheria: What percentage of submissions are just junk vs. really good.

Mystery editor: Roughly 80 percent or more ... wait a minute, dusting off from lightning strike. Thanks, Jan.

Mystery editor: And in that "junk" pile are included poorly targeted manuscripts. For example nonfiction to a publisher who only does fiction. There's some really wacky stuff out there and some with just really poor writing, but a lot of it is just not THERE yet. Too weak to save. No vital signs.

estheria: Who actually reads unsolicited submissions?

Rebe: Is it true that the first person to read manuscripts in the slush pile is not an editor but rather an administrative assistant, a college intern, or another person in the office? If that person does not care for the manuscript, then an editor never even sees it?

Mystery editor: It depends. Usually there is a first reader whose job is to weed out that 80 percent plus. Don't discount interns and assistants. They sometimes will give you more attention than the overworked editor. My assistant has pulled stuff out that I was about to discard. Really.

Mystery editor: Somebody has to weed the garden before the editor goes out to pick the tomatoes. Otherwise, the editor can't FIND the tomatoes. On the average, only 10 to 15 percent of the slush is edible (if you want to continue with the gardening analogy). Five percent or less is appetizing. One percent or less winds up on a plate (published). You can't eat it all no matter how tasty it is. The first reader, who may be an intern or assistant, gets rid of the weeds ... the stuff that is poorly targeted, poorly written, obviously not right for the house. I would not poo-poo interns or assistants. Generally speaking, they have less responsibilities, less to do. They are a little fresher, a little less jaded. They also know who at the house likes what and when is the best time to show somebody something. Lower-rung people want to be higher-rung people. One of the ways they do that is to prove they have "a good eye," and are able to pick good manuscripts. Interns are wanting to learn, so they spend a little more time reading than someone who has a million other things to do besides reading manuscripts. Don't diss interns.

estheria: If a manuscript had been favorably critiqued by an editor at a SCBWI conference, should that be mentioned in a query/cover letter to another editor when sending out that particular manuscript? Would it make you read it a little more carefully knowing this writer is serious enough to attend a writer's conference and pay for a critique?

Mystery editor: Nah, I wouldn't. It's all subjective. It's the story that counts. HOWEVER, if you are sending it to the editor who critiqued it, then by all means YES, do some memory jogging.

Army: I would love to know if having an agent is the key to breaking out of the slush pile.

Mystery editor: It helps. Generally agented subs go to editors directly. You've passed quality control. But it's not a guarantee of getting published. Also, a good agent will know which editor is looking for what.

Mystery editor: Get a reputable agent. A bad agent is worse than no agent. There are some agents whose stuff I won't even look at because the agent isn't professional. Look for someone who is selling to closed houses. Check them out on Preditors and Editors.

Mystery editor: Let me repeat—make sure you sign with a reputable, respectable agent. There are folks out there who aren't evil. They are just clueless. They sub material that isn't ready to be subbed. They don't write effective cover or query letters. They don't know how to follow up properly. In short, they sub with about as much know-how as the average new children's book writer. Editors are just going to ignore these people, and subs from them will go in the trash. You want to go with an agent who has the ability to get you into a closed house. Otherwise, just do the work yourself.

scribe: What's the number one thing you wish writers knew?

Mystery editor: One thing? Only one thing? Okay, a moment for thought. See some writers need to know different things from other writers.

Jan: Can you think of one thing that would help if every writer knew it?

Mystery editor: I think the theme in all the questions I answered offline for Jan was to think of writing for children as a profession. You probably will need another profession to support this one. But be professional. And write for the love of it. The pursuit of publication can tarnish the passion that you need to get published in the first place. There's a catch-22 for you. Believe in your own writing and keep improving your craft.

Mystery editor: Oh dear, that was so a Hallmark moment.

Jan: I've got one ... I've got one ... I've got one ... "Not every good book will get published (sorry), but every good writer will get published if you don't give up on your work and you keep trying."

Mystery editor: Yes! Yes! That's it! I was thinking of that every good book thing today and couldn't articulate it quite like I wanted. Don't put all your eggs on one story ... umm, one basket.

Jan: Some writers invest too much in the one manuscript ... you have more stories in you; sell the next one if this one isn't working for editors right now.

Mystery editor: You are typing faster than I can think, Jan. I agree. Yes.

Mystery editor: Oh, I know. Besides the treating writing as a profession and not a hobby, realize there is room for improvement, and writing well is learned. Early efforts are not an indication of whether you can write or not. I've heard other editors compare writing to the Olympics. That's a common analogy. There's a growth and learning period. Don't give up. And like Jan said, write more. Diversify. It's a numbers game. The more chips you have in the ring, the better off you are or something. I do not gamble.

Mystery editor: There that was at least FIVE things.

scribe: What do you think of bilingual picture books? Would there be a good market for them or would publishers have some reservations to offer them to children at this age?

Mystery editor: This is a specialty thing, and you should submit to houses specifically interested in that sort of thing. But then I guess it depends on HOW bilingual ... if your story is strong ... with mass market appeal ... and you have a bilingual thing going ... it could work.

Rebe: What young/first-time authors publishing today would you identify as having the potential to be among the next great generation of writers for children and young adults?

Mystery editor: Cynthia Lord, Kate DiCamillo, Lisa Yee, Jennifer Choldenko (I may be stretching your definition of today and first time ... I'm thinking relatively new on the scene). There are many really amazing first-time novels I'm thinking of, but the titles are eluding my brain.

ehill: Is it all about timing? The writer/agent has sent you an absolutely GREAT adventure book manuscript for middle-grade readers. However, it missed your "deadline" for the season. You had already agreed to publish another adventure book that fit the market needs in that category. Is the GREAT "rejected" manuscript automatically in your slush pile or will it have any chances for future publication in your publishing house?

Mystery editor: I'm not going to hold onto something that we won't be ready to contract for years. It's one of those sad things and one of those hard rejections to write. Generally, I tell the person the truth. Love it. Can't take it. Already have one. Or it depends if there is an opening in the next list, but generally it probably is just one of those bad timing things. The other adventure story would not have been accepted if it was not stellar or did not fill a niche.

Jan: And some writers don't realize that a book will be on the publisher's list for more than a year—maybe for more than a couple years, so you really aren't looking at waiting a year and trying again. Because the publisher still isn't going to want a book that competes with the one they still market.

Mystery editor: Yes. It would be too long. And I wouldn't want to hold something up. It just isn't going to work for us. Storylines can be so similar. People worry about ideas getting lifted. But there are very few stories that I haven't already seen a version of.

Jillp: I was wondering what the editor thought about incorporating mathematics in middle-grade fiction.

Specifically, the fiction would be a mystery that revolves around math clues.

Mystery editor: That sounds excellent. With all the standards-based educational trends this would be a marketing plus.

Craymom: How does print compete with technology?

Mystery editor: That's a question that we'll see the answer to as time goes by. If you are talking about ebooks, I don't see paper books going away anytime soon. If you are talking about techno gadgets competing for children's attention— that is something for teachers and parents to pay attention to. The kids I know—the kids I see—are still book readers. As long as there are good books, kids are still going to grab them up. I hope so or there goes my job.

Jan: Studies show that kids still read ... a lot actually. Teens read a lot too, but so much of it is for school that they don't do as much pleasure reading. It's the adults who are slacking off on the reading ... they score the lowest in daily reading hours. So ... y'all read now!

Craymom: Does it deter an editor to receive a submission from an overseas writer?

Mystery editor: No, it doesn't matter as long as there isn't a language barrier.

crafty: When you get to the end of a query letter, what contact information do you want to see? I have an address, land line phone #, cell phone #, email, fax, etc. I could add but that seems like a lot of stuff. What do you actually want/need?

Mystery editor: All of that. If one doesn't work I have another to rely on. You wouldn't believe how many times authors send bad email addresses. Fax, maybe not. Address, email, at least one phone number. Things are slow, you might move or something. Please include more than one method of contact.

c-yo: With simultaneous subs should you let editors know you are simultaneously subbing?

Mystery editor: Yes, please do. It's a courtesy. It's a pain to spend a lot of time working on and reviewing something and then finding out it's gone somewhere else. Many editors compare publishing to dating so, yes, we like to know if we are going steady or not.

chuffchuff: Once a manuscript catches the interest of an editor, is there anything a writer can do to promote the story through the selection pyramid aside from hope? What is the acquisition process at your house?

Mystery editor: No, it's out of your hands at that point. The acquisition process is too complicated and we are running low on time.

writermaw: I was a lover of the Judy Blume books growing up. *Deenie* was one of my favorites. There was a lot of controversy over some parts of it. Are editors getting more/less strict in what is published in kids' books today?

Mystery editor: Times have changed so what was a problem THEN is not a problem now. Again it depends on the publisher. Some smaller publishers might have a more niche focus.

tagsale: When you see "sim sub" (simultaneous submission) are you more or less interested?

Mystery editor: Neither. It's a good thing to know. And it gives me a flag to wave at acquisitions. As in a good flag to wave. Hello, Boss, this is a sim sub. Lookee NOW! But I have to have already fallen in love.

Mystery editor: As to sim subs ... if you have already entered conversation with an editor as in they have responded to you ... and there is contact, tell them if you get a nibble, I usually ask people to do that if I've taken or am taking it to acquisitions.

c-yo: Where can a writer look to find projected topic trends?

Mystery editor: I don't know if they can. Trends are so trendy. Watch what is coming out. But the trends change by the time the book hits the shelf.

Scribemom: What about a book/stuffed animal concept? Acceptable?

Mystery editor: Unless the publisher actually WANTS that, I'd let that be something that is brought up when you've entered the acquisition or contract phase.

Jan: Also, novelty packaging like that requires a lot more money outlay. So, you might want to look at the publishers who seem to be doing it.

Sandra: We as writers spend so much time stressing over them, just how important is the cover letter? What should it include? And is cleverness and creativity frowned upon when you're forming one?

Mystery editor: This is an individual preference thing, and editors have quirks. I've heard all kinds of different viewpoints at conferences. Generally, short, sweet, and professional. A dab of personality does help. Just don't get too cutesy or act like a used car salesman.

But yeah a dab of cleverness and creativity can be a good thing. Think of your cover letter as your initial job interview. A QUERY letter is a different animal ... that's more of a sales tool. You aren't sending in your manuscript ... you are trying to hook the editor on the query alone. There are tons of sites that show you how to write one of those.

Scribemom: What is happening to the picture book market?

Mystery editor: It's up, it's down, it's all around. Seriously, I think it's picking up. The thing is, EVERYBODY thinks picture books are easy to do. So tons of people do them. The competition is very, very stiff. If you really want to write picture books, zero in and study that genre.

Sunshine: Do kids read chapter books anymore?

Mystery editor: Yes ... if you mean the transition between early readers and middle grade novels.

Scribemom: What is the "hook" needed to get a contract?

Mystery editor: Well, you put bait on a hook to lure a fish, right? And you need the right bait and hook to lure the fish you want. So in a manuscript, your hook has to be that thing that grabs the editor ... makes them bite. Think about your own thought process when you are choosing a book to read. What hooks you? That's what you need in your own manuscripts.

kimber: Since not every good book is definitely going to sell to a publisher, would you ever recommend self-publishing?

Mystery editor: If you really believe in it, and you really want to spend the time and money, go for it. Educate yourself on that though. I wouldn't give up on traditional publishing if one manuscript does not fly. And keep trying other markets, exhaust your possibilities before shelving a manuscript, or maybe wait for trends to change.

Jan: You kind of have to make a decision on whether you want to be a writer, in which case you just keep writing until you make the connection for a sale Or if you want to switch to being a bookseller, press agent, designer ... and a bunch of other jobs for one book. Because self-publishing (if done well) is incredibly consuming, and you won't be writing if you're doing it.

Estheria: Do you have an eye on any emerging/under-represented markets.

Mystery editor: Sometimes we are on the lookout for something we don't have. We have sort of our own niche—aren't really trend followers but that doesn't mean others aren't.

Jan: She also wants to know if there are any less competitive markets.

Mystery editor: Yes, nonfiction which our house publishes very little of. Picture books are glutted. It's hard to shine.

Mystery editor: You know what I would like to see more of? Stories where the kids don't have so many problems. I mean there is the plot problem, but the kid also has divorced parents, a lesbian sister, an amputated limb, and a speech impediment. I think writers think edgy means putting a lot of PROBLEMS in there, and it detracts from the plot. I'd like to see more stories with living parents who are married to each other. Seriously. Too many dead, divorced, estranged parents. It's become the norm.

Jan: I think people don't really have an understanding of how much slush publishers get. Can you give us a number and amount of time as an example ... like ... 500 in a month or whatever?

Mystery editor: Approximately 800 a month. 150-200 a week, at least. More after New Year's ... those darn resolutions.

Jan: That's a lot of things to read when you also have a completely full set of other duties.

Mystery editor: Yes, and slush is not a priority, which I think writers do not understand. Slush can be overwhelming. You ask for gemstones and they deliver unpolished rocks. You have to dig through all those rocks to find your gem. So you end up going to a gem dealer, otherwise known as an agent. Or you have more manuscripts than you can handle, your list fills up, so you close to unsolicited.

sparton: What should you do if you get the response, "If you could send me some of your published clippings, I'd love to consider your story." I have no published clippings yet.

Mystery editor: I'd write up the best sample I could think of and say, "I'm not published but here are some samples." Then I'd work on getting some clippings for the next time you get that response.

Jan: Oh, someone wants to know if editors ever hang out on message boards and mailing lists ... oh yes! I've met really nice editors on message boards and mailing lists. And you visit boards when you have time, right?

Mystery editor: Yes, editors do. It's a way to stay connected. And editors like to relax also. Also many writers take jobs as first readers, interns, or assistants. I'd highly recommend that if you get the opportunity.

Jan: How do you get a first reader job?

Mystery editor: Watch for job openings. I've known some people who have done it because of personal contact. I think *Publishers Weekly* lists openings. If you have an established relationship you can always ask if an internship is available.

Marget: Can an effective book proposal simply be an outline and sample chapters?

Mystery editor: I'm not sure what you mean by this. Are you talking about nonfiction? If so, I'm not that familiar with nonfiction proposals, since my house doesn't publish nonfiction. If you are talking about fiction, you should follow the publisher's guidelines. Send what they ask you to send.

Sheret: Do editors look for high concept books when trudging through their piles?

Mystery editor: If those are the type of manuscripts they wish to publish, yes. I'd study the publisher's catalog to get a feel for what that house publishes. Some houses might prefer something more literary. Acquiring manuscripts is like furnishing a house. You are going to pick what matches your style and what goes well with what you already have.

hideme: In picture books, do editors prefer the main character to be animal or human?

Mystery editor: Depends on the editor/house. Some editors say NO to talking animals ... just because there is an overabundance of overly cutesy, poorly written talking animal manuscripts floating around.

hideme: Although, I'm sure it can vary from publishing house to publishing house, what type of subject matter are editors looking for this year?

Mystery editor: Wow, the year just got started. That's a really hard question to answer, because the old adage, "We don't know what we are looking for until we see it," is basically true. Editors are always on the lookout for fresh, well-written stories.

kimber: I was wondering how someone starts on the road to publication. I've had zero experience, except for a few small poetry competitions at school and online. I'm also still a teen, and I wondered if I could use that to my advantage. Basically, where and how should I begin?

Mystery editor: Congrats on wanting to start down the road early. Where to begin ... look at it like any other profession. If you are still in high school/college gain experience with publications—newspapers or literary magazines. Read, read, read, read, and READ. There is a plethora of info on the web. Some teen writers have become very popular, but the most important thing is writing a good story, regardless of your age.

Marcy: What are editors looking for specifically in a cover letter?

Mystery editor: Short. Simple. Professional. Different editors have quirks ... so if you get to a conference or read an online interview, pay attention to that. Basically, be professional. You can put a little personal spin on it, but be professional. I don't need to know your sob story ... how much your kids like the story ... don't tell me how I'm going to FEEL about your story ... I like to figure that out. Only include RELEVANT background info. Do not appear aggressive or desperate. Don't bring up advance or other payment in the cover letter. Professional. Editors get clues about what it would be like to work with you from your cover letter.

Marcy: What is popular and selling these days?

Mystery editor: It's hard to say. Don't go by trends. By the time you sub something, it's accepted and published, the trend is long gone. You can best get an idea by studying recent releases. Study publisher catalogs.

Marcy: What is the best way to sell our manuscripts to editors?

Mystery editor: Carefully study the market. Make sure you are writing on a professional level before subbing. Follow directions. Read, read, read, read, read. Write, write, write, write, write. It's a numbers game.

Marcy: How do we reach the top of the pile and into the door?

Mystery editor: You write from your heart, only the story you can tell. And you become a masterful story teller. It's a very subjective business. Study the market. Learn. Don't write in a vacuum.

MaryS: What has happened to fairy tales?

Mystery editor: I'm not sure what you mean. Very, very long picture books with morals are out of vogue ... if you are talking about why the old-fashioned traditional fairy tale doesn't get published. I see a TON of retold fairy tales in the slush pile. If you are going to do that, try the lesser known fairy tales. I've seen the Cinderella story in every conceivable form. Frogella, Slugella, etc.

Rebecca: If you are not totally grabbed by the first page, how much farther in a fiction manuscript are you likely to read?

Mystery editor: If I'm not totally grabbed by the first page, then I'm not reading any farther. I may not get beyond the first paragraph or even the first sentence. When it comes to rhyming picture books, the first time I think "ouch!" because of the rhyme and meter, it's gone. There are too many to choose from. Think about when you go to the store to buy a sweater. There are hundreds of sweaters on the rack. How much time do you spend looking at the ones which are not in a color or style you like, which are the wrong size, which do not appeal to you for any reason, ... you don't. You don't have the time. You spend your time looking for want you want. Another thing, maybe you see a sweater that is very beautiful ... unique ... snazzy even ... but it has a major flaw or two or three ... missing buttons, pulled threads, a rip ... you COULD fix it up ... but that would be a lot of work ... and, hey, there's another sweater over there that you like just as much ... maybe a tad more ... and it's in perfect shape!

Flounder2: What is the best way to find publishers who are interested in the type and style of material that I am currently working on? I am basically an unpublished writer.

Mystery editor: Study their catalogs. Browse their web sites. Attend conferences or look for interviews online or in any of the various publications. Join message boards, where other writers share information about editors.

More on publishers: Understand what a traditional publisher does. Do not confuse a traditional publisher with a printer, a vanity press, or an agent. A traditional publisher is in the business of selling books, not in the business of putting writer's works in print. Yes, it crosses over at some point, but the big thing is, Will it sell? Will it make the publisher money? Will it bring the publisher prestige? Will it get awards? Is it worth the investment? Will the book earn enough to pay for how much it costs to produce PLUS make a profit. It's not all artsy angels in the clouds with gilded quill pens. It's business. It's fine and dandy if your relatives, friends, and co-workers like your book when you read it to them. BUT ... are they willing to pay $15-$20 for it?

craftymom: Are serious issues like the things teens go through during puberty too "mature" for a teen story? Several people I know were doing stuff they shouldn't have back in high school and I know lots of bad examples, the trouble they caused, and the lessons those people learned. Too heavy?

Mystery editor: No, not too heavy. Just make sure you have a STORY, and it's not a long list of things that happen. Don't make it preachy. I don't know when you were a teen, but make it current for teens today.

craftymom: When is the best time of year to submit?

Mystery editor: I don't think there is a better or best time. Manuscripts can hang out in a slush pile for weeks or months, so just go ahead and get them in the stack.

craftymom: I know that multiple submissions all at once are a no no, but what if I have multiple things to submit? Should I send one, wait a few days, send another, and so on?

Mystery editor: Send one at a time. Wait to hear back on one before you send another. You could get valuable feedback from the first that will help you on the second. If you want stuff out there, send to different publishers. Don't pepper one with a bunch of manuscripts.

Cy-2: Which boards do editors visit?

Mystery editor: I think you can find them just about everywhere. Some are open about who they are. Some lurk. Some have personas.

Mar127: I have sometimes been required to produce a chapter-by-chapter outline in addition to a synopsis. In every case, I have found my characters leading me in a different (and usually more creative) direction. I would be interested in your feelings about outlines in terms of plot development.

Mystery editor: If things shift—fine. Usually what an editor wants to see with the chapter outline is that you have thought the story out—that it's done.

chuffchuff: As a new writer, should one submit a resume with work?

Mystery editor: No need to unless the guidelines ask for that. I think some educational publishers do.

frostyboy: What other pub resources are useful?

Mystery editor: Internet. Writers' magazines. There are several around.

Jan: Um ... stuff here at <u>Institute of Children's Literature</u>. And the annuals we publish are amazing.

writerz: what are the rules involved with writing stories based on nonfiction "reality" television shows?

Jan: I'll catch this one. You can't do it without permission—— which a big publisher might secure if they loved the book but it's going to make it that much harder to sell. BUT, I have seen books with reality shows in the plot—but they were made-up reality shows.

writerz: What's the average turnaround time to receive a response from a submission?

Mystery editor: Depends on the workload at the publisher and the amount of slush. Varies from publisher to publisher.

writerz: Is there a market for children's poetry?

Mystery editor: Yes. It's not booming, but it's there.

chuffchuff: Have you ever seriously considered a manuscript you reviewed at a writers' conference?

Mystery editor: Yes. We've even bought them.

kimber: What about classic writing (like the style of *Anne of Green Gables*)? Is there still a market?

Mystery editor: *Take Me Out to the Ball Game* is no longer on the Top 40 hits list, and writing styles that were popular last century are not popular today. *Anne of Green Gables* was published 100 years ago. You should write like someone who lives in this century. Austen and Dickens (as is) would probably no more be published in this century, than Judy Blume and Doreen Cronin would be in the 1800s. If you want to write a historical story set in the same time as *Anne of Green Gables*, yes. And anytime you write, you want the voice and dialogue to match the story you are telling. (I'm not sure a medieval princess would be using contemporary street slang.) But, yes, writing produced today can become as classic as the Anne stories. I have seen books with that old-fashioned flair. *The Miraculous Journey of Edward Tulane* by Kate DiCamillo comes to mind. But like DiCamillo, you might have to already break in before you can get something like that published.

writermaw: How many Mark Twains have you come across in your career (meaning "natural" talent, unique, and not trained)?

Mystery editor: If somebody sends in an incredible story, I have no idea whether it came "naturally" or they spent 20 years honing their voice. No matter how much talent you have, I think there is always room for improvement, and the field is much more competitive than it was in Twain's day. In addition, things are more commercial, and a lot of getting published depends on how marketable things are.

91

Mousy: What do you think will be the next trend in children's lit?

Mystery editor: Don't worry about trends. Write YOUR stories. By the time you follow trends, the trend has changed. It could take up to a year from the time you submit until the publisher issues the contract. Then another one to three years in production. And by then a new trend. There is always a need for fresh, incredible stories.

hazydazy: What percentage of that slush is truly unpublishable?

Mystery editor: This has to be the most frequently asked question in this chat. Stop worrying about it. Less than one percent of the slush pile will typically be published—at THAT house. That's why you have to send the manuscript to every house that is a MATCH for that manuscript. Keep working on your craft, and get yourself in that top five percent quality-wise. It's also why you need to write more than one story, and one or more genre or style if you have that flexibility. If you wanted to be a baker, but you only learned to bake one kind of cake, well, you probably would not flourish in business.

Jan: I want to thank you for coming out and the INCREDIBLE amount of time you put into answering ALL the email questions.

6 _____

Jan Fields' List Of Five Good Tools That Can Get You Into Bad Trouble

Doing a good job without the proper tools can be tough. But it's even harder to do a good job with tools used improperly or without care. A hammer can be invaluable for driving a nail but can also punch a whole in the wall and mash your finger. So learning to use your tools in a controlled manner is important. It's important for building a house. And it's important for building a story or article. Being careless with a tool or using it for the wrong job can seriously wreck your results. Let's look at some commonly misused writing tools.

1. Thesaurus

I love the thesaurus. I don't use it very often, but when I'm hunting for just the right word and it refuses to bubble up from my cheese brain, the thesaurus has saved me more than once. But a thesaurus is only as good as your understanding of the words it offers.

The thesaurus groups related words, words whose meanings are similar—but not exact. Words are unique items. "Run" and "trot" are synonyms, but they aren't strictly interchangeable. If you write, "Jack ran up the hill," you have a totally different feel and nuance than if you say, "Jack trotted up the hill." A trot is more leisurely, more fun, more light-hearted than a run. And of course, if you're choosing the gait for a horse, a trot and a run are very different indeed.

I often see reckless thesaurus use in manuscripts and so do editors. This happens when a writer knows that he/she doesn't want a tepid little verb like "went" or "moved" but then used the thesaurus and grabs a word without thought to what else it might be carrying.

Words carry more than definition; they get the extra baggage of attitude. For example, among movement words "ambled" has an entirely different attitude than "shuffled" and many times I've seen one of these used in entirely the wrong mood.

While the thesaurus has coaxed many writers into poor choices for words for movement, it's done far more harm when writers pick wildly in choosing words for speech tags. Think about it a moment. When you're describing how you told your husband about the fender bender this morning, were you tempted to tell him you "decried," "queried," "equivocated," or "conjectured?" If not, why use them?

Unexpected words that don't flow with the style of the rest of your narration draw attention away from the content of your story/article and onto the word. It's like wearing a beautiful outfit with a dirty rag tied around your wrist. The part that "doesn't fit" will draw the eye and distract from the image you're trying to convey. So don't choose words you wouldn't casually use—don't reach way beyond your real working vocabulary or you'll have a sudden shift in voice that calls a halt to the reader's momentum and makes him wonder why this thing is there.

2. Spell check

Spell check is a great thing as it helps me catch a lot of my typos—not all of them, but a lot. I would really miss having spell check if it went away. But I know better than to rely upon it too heavily. Spell check won't catch usage errors (and grammar check doesn't do much better with those, so don't think clicking that on will save you some serious proofreading).

But spell check will not help you choose the correct word if you don't know it already. When I type "I ate supper at there home," spell check is perfectly content with that. It doesn't flag it. It doesn't try to get me to make the change. That's because it knows "there" is a word, and it doesn't know that "there" is not the correct word. I need to know that.

So if you have word choice weaknesses, if you have trouble telling when to say "its" and when to say "it's," or you tend to use the word "to" when you mean "too," or if you find you are unsure of the right times to use affect/effect, lay/lie, or then/than—stop, drop, and learn. Look them up, write out the rules, and tape them to your computer monitor or other obvious place so you can see them every single time you revise. Spell check can't do that for you—but it still needs to be done.

3. Market guide

A market guide is a wonderful thing, and we even create two of our own at <u>Institute of Children's Literature</u> that we give away with our courses. It can point us toward markets we haven't considered. It can be a great place to check our memory for details of that market. But if used incorrectly it can cause you to make inappropriate submissions that annoy editors.

Just because a book market guide list hundreds of publishers doesn't mean there are literally hundreds of publishers who might publish your specific book. It also doesn't mean there are hundreds of publishers you would even consider letting publish your book.

I have heard authors say, "I send a query to everyone, and if I get any nibbles, I'll start researching the ones that seem interested." Why? Why would you clog up an already explosive slush pile with one more inappropriate submission just because you don't want to bother researching? Is your time worth so little? Do you feel the editor's time is worth so little? Do you want to encourage more publishers to close the door to submissions?

The market guide can seem a little alarming. There are a lot of publishers in there. That's why I tend to approach it in two ways. First, I tackle a few pages at a time when I get a new market guide, and I read every single thing about a publisher on those few pages. I read whether they publish fiction or nonfiction (really this is basic and an amazing number of writers skip that one simple item). I read their age groups, word lengths, and departments. I read everything, and if a market seems like a likely one for me, I highlight that market in my guide so I can learn more about it by tracking it down online.

The second thing I do with my market guide is to use it as the STARTING PLACE when I have a piece ready to sell. I use the INDEX to look for markets that publish the sort of project I'm submitting. There is no point in my sending a picture book to Llewellyn FLUX, for example, since they only publish YA. And yet—I would be willing to bet they get picture book submissions. But I don't have time to waste on pointless submissions.

When I have used the index to make a list of likely markets, I read every single one of the likely market entries from first word to last. I'm looking for any reason why this market definitely wouldn't publish my project. Do they only take resumes/clips—then no point sending them a finished project, and I strike them off my list. Do they only take nonfiction and this is a fiction project—then I strike them off my list. Finally, I look at the remaining possibilities and I move beyond the market guide to find out if this is really a possible market before I send anything. From this point I:

a) Use Google to check for the publisher's web site which I read entirely, making notes of anything I learn.

b) Continue down the Google links to read things people have written about the publisher—am I finding complaints or warnings? This will definitely move them off my list. I'm a writer, not a gambler.

c) If this is a book project, I continue to Google so I can find links to book reviews or links to the publisher's authors. I want to find out if this publisher is getting books reviewed and I want to see cover images. Professional covers look professional and that will tell me a lot about whether I want to deal with that publisher.

d) If this is a book project, I take my list (which now has several titles by each publisher) to my big box bookstore and try to find books by that publisher. If the bookstore has NONE of the publisher's titles and they can only be gotten by special order, I mark them off my list. I am not interested in selling books out of my car, I need the publisher to place the books in bookstores so the professionals can sell them.

4. Your computer

So how can your computer get you into trouble? Many writers simply don't know how to use it. They don't know how to do headers. They don't know how to set margins. Or worse still, they know too much and decide to make the manuscript format suit their own aesthetics with homemade illustrations pasted in, fully justified margins, and fancy fonts and sizes.

Computers are both too hard and too easy. Many writers just give up on learning the basics of setting margins, making headers, and setting spacing. So writers are still double-spacing by hitting "enter" twice at the end of every line and typing in headers on each page and hoping they don't migrate too much when they begin revising. This will eventually do you a huge amount of harm in selling your work professionally.

Learn to do those basic things in your computer. If you can't figure out your help file, find a helpful teenager to explain it to you. Find someone who can show you. Consider it as essential as any other aspect of learning to write.

You know that market guide I warned you about—chances are it has a section near the beginning of the guide that shows you what a finished manuscript should look like. It will show you what headers, what margins, what spacing, etc., you should use. Use those. Editors won't be impressed by your cute manuscript—they'll be impressed by your great writing. A cute manuscript will just annoy. Don't make your writing compete with the annoyance of a "choose your own formatting" manuscript.

Conquer your computer. It's time. Really.

5. Your enthusiasm

Okay, how can your enthusiasm *possibly* get you into trouble? It can push you to hurry. I hate to break it to you but writing is not a good profession for people in a hurry. The editor won't be in a hurry. The publisher won't be in a hurry. So you need to calm down and refuse to hurry too. Take the time to get it right.

If you've heard yourself say, "I don't know much about grammar, but I can tell a good story," it's time to learn about grammar or get yourself an excellent critique partner with a lot of patience. Because the competition is fierce. (And if you're self-publishing, you may sell your book at first, but a well-written story will continue to sell, as well as get good reviews.) An editor doesn't have to take a good story with bad grammar because she already has five good stories with good grammar competing for that publishing spot. An editor doesn't have to deal with trying to read a single-spaced manuscript, or guess at your word count because you didn't read about what needed to be in a header—she already has a pile of good stories by writers who took the time to learn how to format a manuscript.

So, if you can tell a great story, that's totally fantastic. Now learn how to do it well. Learn how to showcase it in a manuscript formatted according to the standard an editor expects to see. Really, you've done the hard part—you told a good story. Don't quit now that you're in the homestretch.

Don't hope the story wows the editor so much she's willing to overlook the stuff you know ... really, you know you needed to do before sending it. Instead, stop and learn to do it all.

And when you're looking at your name in print and thinking about all the children reading your words and benefiting from them, you'll be glad you took the time to control your tools. I know you will.

7 _____

CHECKLISTS

Your Organization Checklist

☐ My story has the three-part structure: beginning, middle, and ending.

• The key to organization is planning. Link the three parts.

☐ I use specific details rather than generalizations.

• Kids will learn new concepts with precise information.

☐ I have an enticing opening.

• Catch your readers early or you will lose them.

☐ My conclusion links to my opening or title.

- A story is like a gift -- it's more significant when you wrap it up.

☐ I use a variety of story components.

- Use analogy, hyperbole, onomatopoeia, etc., with dialogue, narration, thoughts, and description.

☐ My story is age-appropriate.

- Make sure both theme and content would interest your target group.

☐ The title entices the reader to continue.

- Have an interesting title, but don't give away the ending.

☐ The plot contains a significant conflict and strong obstacles.

- Insignificant conflicts and obstacles do not maintain youthful interest.

Characters and Settings Checklist

- ☐ I show, rather than tell about, my characters and setting.

- Telling a story sounds like a lecture to a child.

- ☐ I present a single point of view.

- Only write what your main character can see, hear, feel, say, do, and think.

- ☐ My characters have unique personalities.

- Readers should be able to easily distinguish between characters.

- ☐ My characters' dialogue moves the story along.

- Each word a character says should reveal plot or characterization.

- ☐ My character(s) grows throughout the story.

- Readers will not identify with characters who do not learn from their mistakes.

- ☐ The adult characters hover in the background.

- Kids want stories about kids solving their own problems.

- ☐ I use sensory imagery.

- Use all five senses to develop setting and characterization.

Sentence Structure Checklist

☐ I use complete sentences.

• Model proper English for young readers.

☐ I use a varied sentence structure.

• Vary sentence length and configuration.

☐ I use active, rather than passive, voice.

• Passive voice can cause characters to disappear.

☐ I use consistent tenses.

• Pick a tense and stay with it throughout the story.

☐ My subject, verb, and object agree.

• Singular words never agree with plural words.

☐ My pronouns agree with my verbs.

• Be aware of which word your pronoun replaces.

☐ I maintain first, second, or third person throughout the story.

• Never switch between *I* and *she* in your story.

☐ I use transition words to show time or location change.

• Young readers appreciate gentle shifts between paragraphs.

☐ I pruned weedy words from my literary garden.

• Every word should advance your story.

Mechanics Checklist

- [ ] Spelling

- Don't trust spell-check to interpret your connotation. Use a dictionary.

- [ ] Capitalization

- Know the rules and obey them.

- [ ] Punctuation

- Avoid overuse of commas and exclamation points. Properly punctuate dialogue.

- [ ] Manuscript properly formatted.

- Editors appreciate a double-spaced manuscript with one-inch margins.

ABOUT THE INSTITUTE

The Institute for Writers and the associated Institute of Children's Literature have taught over 404,000 students how to write a book for children and get published. This book was compiled and edited by the Director of the Institute, Katie Davis.

Katie Davis's books for children, published by Harcourt, Simon & Schuster, HarperCollins, and Diversion Books, have sold over 755,000 copies. She is also the award-winning author of the Amazon bestseller *How to Promote Your Children's Book*.

Made in the USA
Lexington, KY
28 April 2017